"Ione, w
Michael **asked,** ~~~~
"Do you know how refreshing you are?"

"You mean I'm not as socially suave as your other women." A disappointed pang checked Hermione's earlier giddiness.

He held out his hand and she took it. His fingers laced around hers in reassurance. "I mean you're a breath of fresh air. And there are no other women. Not since you."

"I meant the ones before."

His fingertips rubbed hers. "I didn't come out of a sealed bag, so yes, I have a checkered past that is far less than the media pretends. Let me be honest. I haven't been able to stop thinking of you."

His declaration created a sense of joyous adrenaline, like when she maneuvered a kayak through white water rapids and felt the cold spray on her face as her stomach launched itself up and down. "Me either," she admitted. "Made worse when I found out that I was going to work with you."

"And that I was a playboy you thought used you."

"I didn't have 'be a notch on a bedpost' on my bucket list," she admitted.

Dear Reader,

This book represents another milestone for me, my 30th novel for Harlequin. It's a dream come true to have been with Harlequin for thirty books. There's a picture of me in my teens, on the beach, reading a Harlequin novel. So this moment is truly special and I'm glad you're part of it.

Life is made up of special moments, and Michael and Ione's story is about when two souls realize they complete each other. Ione's more scientific and Michael's more spontaneous, but together they learn that their combined strengths make them unstoppable. They are better together than apart, but it's hard for Ione to trust, especially as she's been burned before. It's easier for her to solve factual problems than to give Michael her heart and be hurt yet again, this time by a man with a playboy reputation.

For *The Playboy Project*, I studied up on endangered bats and bald eagles, both of which feature prominently in the story as they do in my home state. If you're in Missouri from late December to early February, watch for eagles perched in trees near the water's edge. They are glorious to see.

I hope you love Michael and Ione as much as I do. Let me know by visiting my website, micheledunaway.com, where you can also subscribe to my newsletter.

Michele Dunaway

THE PLAYBOY
PROJECT

MICHELE DUNAWAY

Harlequin

SPECIAL EDITION

Harlequin®
SPECIAL
EDITION™

Recycling programs
for this product may
not exist in your area.

ISBN-13: 978-1-335-18002-5

The Playboy Project

Copyright © 2025 by Michele Dunaway

For questions and comments about the quality of this book, please contact us at CustomerService@Harlequin.com.

TM and ® are trademarks of Harlequin Enterprises ULC.

 Harlequin Enterprises ULC
22 Adelaide St. West, 41st Floor
Toronto, Ontario M5H 4E3, Canada
www.Harlequin.com

Printed in Lithuania

MIX
Paper | Supporting
responsible forestry
FSC® C021394

In first grade, **Michele Dunaway** wanted to be a teacher. In second grade, she wanted to be a writer. By third grade, she decided to be both. Now a bestselling contemporary author, Michele strives to create strong heroes and heroines for savvy readers who want contemporary, small-town adventures with characters who discover things about themselves as they travel the road to true love and self-fulfillment. Michele recently retired from an award-winning English and journalism teaching career. She loves to travel, with the places she visits often inspiring her novels. She's a mom of two grown daughters and several rescue cats. (The cats, of course, completely rule the roost.) An avid baker, Michele describes herself as a woman who does way too much but never wants to stop, especially when it comes to creating fiction, or baking brownies and chocolate chip cookies. Her website is micheledunaway.com.

Books by Michele Dunaway

The Fortunes of Texas:
Secrets of Fortune's Gold Ranch

Conveniently a Fortune

Harlequin Special Edition

Love in the Valley

What Happens in the Air
All's Fair in Love and Wine
Love's Secret Ingredient
One Suite Deal
Room for Two More
The Playboy Project

Visit the Author Profile page
at Harlequin.com for more titles.

Chapter One

Birds and bees he could deal with. Michael Clayton knew them well, if the vicious internet gossips plastering his supposed sexcapades online were to be believed. But bats? Real, live, endangered bats a mere three inches long with wingspans of ten to twelve inches? The fact that Michael had bats on the brain was entirely the fault of his environmentally conscious older brother, Liam. Well, his eldest brother, Edmund was also at fault, since it was his abdication of his position as CEO of the family company that had landed Michael here. But mostly it was Liam's fault for insisting Clayton Holdings work in harmony with nature and not against it.

Michael would have read Liam the riot act—that was, if Liam wasn't circulating through the crowd of wedding guests there to celebrate his nuptials. In a surprise ceremony, Liam had married Lexi in the solarium of their parents' house. Even Michael knew he couldn't interrupt his happily married brother with a small problem of an endangered species, at least not until *after* the honeymoon.

"You're frowning," Eva said as she tipped a champagne flute toward him. The youngest of the four Clayton siblings glittered in her blue sequined gown. Even at a petite five-two, she held her own against her three older brothers. "This is a happy occasion. You should be smiling. You know, use the teeth Mom and Dad paid a fortune to straighten."

"I was thinking," Michael snapped.

Eva lifted a perfectly arched dark eyebrow, a movement she'd perfected long ago and used to good advantage. "That can be dangerous where you're concerned."

A little dig, and perhaps one Michael deserved, especially after needing his sister to extract him from the latest online gossip. This scandal, however, had not been his fault. Well, not technically. In the court of public opinion, he had done the crime and earned the time. He simply didn't like the length of his penance, or his self-imposed banishment from the Portland society he'd enjoyed so well.

"Gee, thanks." He sipped champagne from the full flute he hadn't touched since Edmund had given the best man's toast. Edmund's defection from the family firm six months ago was the entire reason Michael had been named VP of Clayton Hotels, a position that was driving him batty. Pun intended.

Michael still found it hard to believe that his older brother, who'd been the CEO heir apparent his entire life, had forsaken the job for love. But Edmund had, and he and his girlfriend, Lana, were busy traveling the world…well, when not attending family weddings. Because of Edmund's decision and their father's edict, Michael found himself more out of sorts than he'd been in years. It wasn't that he was in over his head. It was more that he never expected to be a VP in the first place.

But his oldest brother had acted totally out of character and surprised everyone, including him.

Eva's red lips parted with a worried sigh. "Okay, what's wrong? What's got you hot and bothered, besides the fact you accidentally kissed your now ex's best friend and got caught in the act a few weeks ago? Are you sad this is a small family affair with no eligible women for you to hit on?"

Michael bristled. "Why does everyone think I jump from bed to bed? I hate that people label me Mr. Love 'em and Leave 'em. You know that's not me. I might have been a bit of a wild child once, but I am not the man-whore everyone claims."

Once sullied, forever stained, and he hated it. His voice, which had vibrated with harshness, caused her gray eyes—the same color as his own—to widen. He softened his tone. "Sorry. Snapping at you was uncalled for. I'm just frustrated. When will it stop? It's not like I'm a British royal."

Eva placed a gentle hand on his arm. "I'm sorry. The press is merciless, but I suspect what's bothering you is more than the 'oh, you're not my girlfriend Rachel and I'm kissing you' scandal you found yourself in. Talk to me. Do you miss her? Rachel?"

"I haven't missed her since we broke up." A harsh truth that he'd had to face in the bright light of day. Was he as shallow as everyone thought he was? Because the truth was, he didn't miss his ex. Following that logic meant that, in the time they'd been together, his heart hadn't been as involved as his mind might have hoped.

"What does that say about me? Are they right? Am I as awful as the gossips portray? A playboy with no morals?" He shrugged off his sister's hand and took another sip of bubbly.

"Of course not. It's only the cesspool of social media. You have to let all the negativity go. You are none of those things. You care deeply and have one of the most generous hearts I know."

"Thanks." His sister's words soothed him somewhat, but didn't quell his anger. "I'm just mad at myself. Who wouldn't be? I gave you yet another scandal to fix because of my own dumb decisions. When will I learn?"

"I'm not keeping score."

He rolled his eyes. "You should be. You've earned your stripes mopping up my messes."

As the VP of Communications for Clayton Holdings, Eva handled Portland's malicious and scandal-loving social media influencers and gossip with a finesse Michael admired and envied. At twenty-six, she was a formidable force, underestimated by many, but not by him.

"I mop up everyone's messes and eat the gossips for lunch. Yours are no worse than Edmund's. Just different."

"That still doesn't excuse my behavior. I didn't realize that the woman I was kissing wasn't Rachel until a few seconds in. The bad publicity was well deserved. I did kiss her best friend."

Eva's expression softened sympathetically. "How could you have known who it was? You were at a masquerade ball and she told you she'd be dressed as a sexy domino. She didn't tell you that all of her friends were going to be dressed exactly the same, right down to their wigs and the number of spots on their costumes. You figured it out pretty much the moment your lips touched hers. That matters."

"It was still a failure on my part." Something that continued to bother Michael to no end. "What did I think was going to happen? Even if it was Rachel, was I going to back her against a wall in some alcove? I know better!" He resisted the urge to pace or jerk a hand through his hair. "Dad's right. I'm twenty-eight. I need to grow up."

"Well, now that you ran yourself out of Portland, you have no need to go back and forth like you were. You can stay here in Beaumont with the rest of us, and get a real chance for a fresh start. Dad's proud of you for moving the corporate offices earlier than the one-year timeline. Living in Beaumont, as tiny as it is, might be just what you need."

Michael doubted it. Being in the Midwest, in a town that was a tiny dot on the map of Missouri, was nothing like living in Oregon. "Moving here for good feels claustrophobic, as if we've been sucked into small-town Americana."

"You are majorly out of sorts," Eva observed, her lips making a worried pucker. "You have six months left 'til you hit the year mark as VP. You know Dad promised Liam he'd reevaluate the roles he gave both of you when Edmund abdicated and went off to see the world with Lana. You make it that far and you'll be free to do whatever. Especially since you got the corporate office relocated here early, probably faster than Edmund would have done. I know I keep saying that, but it's true and it'll let you do what you want once he comes back and resumes his VP spot."

Not that Michael knew exactly what he wanted to do, anyway. "It's not that." The words came easily, as they had for the past hundred and eighty-two days, not that he was counting. "I like the job. Well, minus the endangered bats and the fact they're making my life miserable."

"You're a good VP."

"I hope so. I'm trying. It's hard to live up to the fact Edmund did both Liam's job and mine." He wanted to be seen as more than a playboy who partied nonstop. He had a head for business, perhaps not as great as Edmund's or his father's, but this was his chance to prove himself. He'd mostly succeeded, until one stupid kiss had undone everything he'd worked for. Another flurry of bad press meant no one cared about Michael's business acumen. No, the gossips were more interested in labeling him a man who couldn't keep his pants zipped. He'd had a decade of this nonsense and invasion into his personal life. His actual relationships were a fraction of what the internet insisted was his tally.

Eva lifted some lint from the sleeve of his tux. "You know I'm here for you. Always."

"Thanks." He gave her a half-hearted smile, one that even he knew didn't meet his eyes. "Means a lot. I'm admittedly out of sorts. A combination of everything, I guess. I'll snap out of it. I always do."

Michael caught sight of Edmund kissing Lana. A pang Michael didn't want to study rushed through him, and he bit the inside of his lip. He was truly grateful to the universe that his brothers had found happiness with the loves of their lives. At the same time, his accomplished older brothers could sometimes be like mirrors reflecting his deficiencies. Not only had he grown up battling their long shadows, but the fact that they were both settled also made it painfully obvious his own life was missing something. He checked the wistful sigh that proved even noted playboys wanted to find true love.

Not that his brothers had ever been playboys. No, that was Michael's fate, and at this point in his life, the reputation rankled. While being called a playboy or a heartbreaker might have been cute when he was younger because of the added mystery and angsty rebellion, he'd tired of the label. Being called a playboy in his late twenties was unwelcome weight, a fixed persona difficult to shed. These days he expected more from himself, so why couldn't others? Why couldn't everyone focus on the good he'd done, rather than his failed relationships? Simple. Because everyone knew good news didn't get clicks.

"It's going to be okay. You and I can be single together for a while," Eva said. "Don't get all broody on me. Weddings are hard for any singletons. Let's drink and make merry. Mom busted out the reserve bubbly, you know, the stuff produced from Dad's first winery."

She was trying to make him feel better, but Michael instead released the sigh he'd been fighting. "Do you ever get bored? Like with how things are? Get up, go to work, go out, go home, repeat." The quick shake of his head sent the black hair that was a gift from their father's side of the family falling onto his forehead. He shoved the strands back and drained the last of the champagne.

"You're sounding like a guy who's having his midlife crisis a few decades early," Eva observed.

"Yeah, no kidding." And he didn't like it. "I've got my Portland condo on the market, the hotel division officially relocated months early, I've moved to Beaumont and our brothers have found their life mates. Where do I fit in?"

"Hanging out with me? I mean, someone's got to do it." Her attempt at humor brought him little cheer.

They both watched as Liam kissed Lexi while gently stroking her stomach, which was round with their twins. Liam and Lexi had met during the opening of the Beaumont Chateau, the premier boutique hotel in the Clayton Holdings portfolio, one Michael oversaw as VP.

Eva sent Michael a wistful smile. "Sometimes it's painful to see our siblings so happy. Makes me feel like I'm missing something. Then I realize that I like my life just fine. I can do what I want, when I want, with who I want, and that's exactly what I want right now."

But what if that wasn't enough? Michael had everything he wanted. Great job. Plenty of money. As much or as little travel as he wanted, with their family's network of hotels as his global playground. He'd never had issues finding a willing woman to grace his arm or his bed, although after a while the women he dated had all seemed like carbon copies of each other.

He couldn't be as shallow as everyone thought. He didn't want to deserve the Portland Playboy name, as he'd been called by the press. At least in the past six months he'd proved the gossips wrong in their beliefs that he didn't do "real work."

As for that work, he'd find a solution to the bats holding up construction of the new hotel. As for the rest? Maybe tonight wasn't the night to figure out his life, or why he felt so alone and melancholy on such a happy occasion. He blinked and refocused on what Eva was saying.

"Beaumont has been good for both Edmund and Liam. Maybe a small town will be a good change of pace for you, too." Eva finished her champagne, then swapped her empty glass for a fresh one as the server circled past.

Michael wanted something far stronger. He tilted his head. "Do you think I'm a small-town type of guy?"

Eva mimicked his gesture, one of her diamond studs winking as she pushed the point of her short bob behind her ear. "No. But maybe it'll surprise you. Besides, St. Louis is forty-five minutes away. And you can always get on a plane. Chris will take you anywhere you need to go, which, frankly, he already does. The question is, where does the VP need to go next?"

"The bar," Michael told her, lightening the moment by finally giving his sister what she called his Hugh Jackman smile because of the way lines crinkled around his eyes. "There's a whiskey calling my name."

But even a drink and two slices of delicious wedding cake didn't settle his restlessness, and he remained in a funk several hours later when he left his parents' house and the reception as soon as it was socially acceptable not to be labeled a party pooper. He drove to historic downtown Beaumont, where three days ago he'd moved into a large two-bedroom apartment located over Joe's Art Gallery on Main Street. He drove slowly toward the two-story building, his teeth rattling as his prized Corvette bumped over the ancient cobblestones that supposedly added to Beaumont's charm. With winter coming, he needed to store his special-edition sports car and buy an SUV. Add not being able to drive his car to the inventory of Beaumont's sins. Gritting his teeth against the self-observation that he sounded like a spoiled, poor little rich brat, he parked behind the art gallery in the building's uncovered lot off the alley. He'd chosen the apartment since its rooftop terrace provided a great view of Beaumont's riverfront park, especially since he missed the Eliot Tower penthouse, where he'd had mountain views during the day and city lights at night. The Portland Art Museum, Farmers Market, shopping and dining had been right outside his front door. In Beaumont, the shops closed by seven at the latest, minus two weekends in September and the week before Christmas. Instead of being the bustling metropolis Michael was used to, the small town's eerie silence was occasionally punctuated by a random car horn, the sound traveling over several miles away from the highway bridge over the Missouri River. He'd been born and raised in a city and found the overall quiet somewhat unnerving.

He made his way to the second floor and turned on the 85-inch TV, which hung on the exposed brick of the open-concept living room. He stripped off his tux and tossed it onto a couch picked out by the designer Eva had hired. His personal possessions would arrive in a week or two, depending on if snowy weather across Utah and Nebraska impeded the path of the moving truck. Not that it mattered when the movers arrived. Like his car, most of his things would go straight into storage until he decided where he wanted to live permanently. For now, the apartment was fine. He poured himself a glass of water and glanced at the clock on the microwave. Not even ten, or eight Portland time. In his current mood, he was going to climb the walls if he stayed home.

Unlike Liam, who loved to climb mountains, the only thing Michael liked to climb into was his bed, and it was too early for that. He should work on Clayton Hotels' bat problem. Instead, he threw on a dark green Henley and blue jeans. Wooden steps thudded under each footfall until he stepped out onto the narrow sidewalk that ran in between his building and the next one, directly to the north. A few steps later he was on Main Street. Beaumont was warmer than normal for Halloween weekend, and no one milled about, minus the group of ghost hunters taking a tour across the street. He walked north, hesitating briefly outside La Vita è Vino Dolce, the self-serve wine bar that he'd visited multiple times… Well, at least until that pretty redhead had gotten the wrong impression and told him she was available.

Before he second-guessed himself for not wanting to chance running in to her, he pushed farther north, toward the town's minuscule bar district. If nothing else, the brisk walk would do him good. Maybe clear his head. Like a beacon, though, a door opened and light and music spilled out of a place he'd never tried. He wasn't wearing a Halloween costume like the people who exited, but he did like the song. He caught the door in his hand and pushed his way inside.

As far as nights went, Ione considered this one a win. Sure, her tour's guests hadn't seen the fabled Woman in White, Beaumont's most famous ghost, but they thankfully didn't seem to mind. Even better, the rain had held off. The mild weather also meant no one shivered and stamped their feet in an attempt to keep warm. The group of twenty instead laughed among themselves and sipped spiked hot chocolate from thermoses, clearly having a good time despite the lack of paranormal activity. Considering that leading guided tours wasn't in her wheelhouse, the night could have been going far, far worse.

Following the directions she'd memorized yesterday, Ione paused in front of the Gratiot House, one of Beaumont's oldest structures. Ione's hometown, which dated back to the late 1700s and the time of Lewis and Clark, had more than one ghost. As the tour was ending, she'd already told stories about the others. She began the rest of the spiel she'd practiced after agreeing to fill in for her sister, Arwen.

"As I said earlier, over one hundred years ago, all the bodies in the small graveyard on Third Street were moved to a larger cemetery outside of town. Even though the Woman in White, as locals call her, is no longer buried here, she's still roaming these streets looking for her lost love." Ione used what Arwen called the conspiratorial whisper, a method of delivery that Arwen had told her would increase the guests' anticipation and add to their experience.

"Now that we're by Gratiot House, be sure to be keep watch as we walk. Our town's most famous ghost likes to make herself known, and she's been seen not only by the town's residents, but also by those on this very tour. You might find her as far away as First Street, where she and her husband once had their business."

Ione pointed dramatically and gave a purposeful shudder. While she wouldn't win any acting awards, her actions did the trick and guests craned their necks. "Her story is tragic. The Woman in White succumbed to cholera shortly after learning her husband had died while exploring the West, and she's still looking for him. Men are especially vulnerable to feeling a tap on the shoulder, but when they turn around, nothing's there!" Ione's voice rose to emphasize her point.

"That's so tragic. She lost her love!" A female tourist's exclamation was accompanied by a full body shiver.

"She did," Ione confirmed, embracing her tour-guide character. She refused to let her sister down. As the group's fearless tour leader, Ione had set the stage by wearing Arwen's costume of black lipstick, heavy black eyeliner, and black clothing. The deep purple felt hat provided a pop of color, although it too was draped in black spider webbing and lace trim.

"She was heartbroken." Ione worked to sell the tale as well as Arwen did. Since it was Halloween and Arwen was busy with the holiday events, she'd asked Ione to take over when her guide had called in sick. In town for the weekend, Ione had agreed to fill in. Her sister's husband had left town on business so he couldn't help.

"Did anyone else feel that?" a guest suddenly cried.

"My EMF reader has something!" another tourist declared, holding out the device so everyone gathered around could see the red and green lights flickering from bottom to top.

"Did it just get colder?" someone else asked.

"I think so!"

"Look over there!"

Ione waited as everyone peered about. She gathered

her scarf closer as a blast of brisk air whipped across the cobblestone streets, carrying chatter with it.

"Does anyone see her?"

"Where did that wind come from?"

Ione knew the truth—the wind came from the Missouri River that formed the eastern edge of the town stuck in time. The TV meteorologist had predicted the cold weather would arrive around midnight, with a one-hundred-percent chance of rain tomorrow. For all its technology, science wasn't perfect. Perhaps the front was arriving early.

Typical of Mother Nature, who, as much as humans tried to predict and control her, always held an ace up her sleeve. This, Dr. Hermione Scott knew well. Ione had a PhD in fish, wildlife and conservation biology from Colorado State University. She loved mountains, forests and streams. The more time she spent outdoors, the better. After a long stint as a wildlife biologist for the US Forest Service, she'd moved into the private sector six months ago, leaving the dark Alaskan winters behind. The shortest amount of daylight in the St. Louis area was nine hours, compared to Fairbanks's whopping three hours and fifty-seven minutes.

"What's that?" A tourist pointed up in the air.

"*Myotis lucifugus*. The little brown bat," Ione told them. "It's the most widespread bat in the country. It's fattening up before it hibernates for the winter."

"That's right. Missouri has a lot of caves," someone added.

"Are we sure it's not Dracula? It is Halloween, after all," someone else said, making the group laugh.

Ione shook her head. No point in telling her group

that this species of bat migrated between summer and winter habitats on a regional scale.

"Is that her?" someone called, and Ione stepped back to let the tour search for the Woman in White. Credited with everything good that happened in Beaumont and blamed for everything bad, the Woman in White had become even more popular after award-winning *Global Outdoors* magazine photographer Shelby Bien Thornton had published her first book of photographs and folklore featuring her hometown. While Ione and Shelby had attended Beaumont High together, they hadn't been in the same grade. Ten years after a breakup during her senior year, Shelby had married her high-school sweetheart, who'd also been the boy next door.

Ione had no high-school sweetheart or current boyfriend. She had an ex whom she'd left in Alaska, an ex who'd done a number on her. Hence her desire to career-build instead of a starting a new relationship.

The wind swirled the dried leaves, and Ione began ushering the group toward the Blanchette Inn, which was owned by Shelby's parents. "Both the inn and Mrs. Thornton's soap shop right next door were once safe spots along the Underground Railroad." Ione paused in the inn's front yard. "This marker pays homage to the early 1800s slaves who chiseled the stones forming the inn's exterior walls and fireplaces. If you listen carefully, you might hear some of their whispers before we go inside, where Mrs. Bien is waiting with hot chocolate and Aunty Jayne's Cookies."

As the group made its way onto the wide front porch, boards creaked and rattled. Large wreaths featuring white ghosts adorned the double front doors. Mrs. Bien made each month's wreaths herself, and she would swap the Halloween theme for a Thanksgiving cornucopia of yellow squashes, tiny orange pumpkins and wooden turkey ornaments. On cue, Mrs. Bien opened the door and welcomed everyone inside.

"Be sure you tell Arwen it was another successful tour," Mrs. Bien said fifteen minutes later as Ione readied to leave. "The guests can't stop talking about it."

"Thank you." The group had been more than generous with their tips. They'd filled the purple hat with large bills, money she'd give Arwen tomorrow. Her sister had already texted that she was going to bed. "Can I do anything to help clean up?" Ione asked.

"No. You go enjoy yourself." Mrs. Bien made a shooing motion.

Married to a city-council member and beloved community icon, Mrs. Bien would send those not staying at the inn on their way soon enough. Arwen's tour company paid both the inn and Aunty Jayne's Cookies a small portion of each ticket price for their roles in the night's adventure. What was that old saying? A rising tide raises all boats? Ione didn't know if that was right, but Beaumont businesses worked to support each other. "Are you doing anything after this?"

"If you don't need me, I'm off to visit with Cordelia," Ione told Mrs. Bien, then she slipped out the door. As Ione walked north on Main, she realized she'd missed Beaumont. A self-professed geek, Ione loved the story of the town's history. The French had been the first Europeans to land on the western edge of the Missouri River, but it had been the wave of German immigrants cultivating grapes who'd later transformed the land now known as Beaumont County. Over two centuries later, area wineries built on that legacy and continued the tradition. Those wineries had caught the attention of the Clayton family, who had purchased almost everything. They'd moved into town, built hotels and brought more tourists into the area, breathing new life into the region.

Ione passed Caldwell's, a bar that had reopened as a makerspace owned by Shelby's husband, Luke. Several years ago, the city council had passed an ordinance requiring liquor sales be less than fifty percent of an establishment's total revenue, and Caldwell's had closed. Cordelia's family bar had made the transition, and Ione grabbed the door handle and entered Kaiser's, a local watering hole popular with the college crowd. Hands out to block random elbows, Ione shoved her way through to the bar where Cordelia was pouring draft beer into multiple glasses. She passed the mugs to a harried server. Seeing Ione slide onto the empty barstool, Cordelia came over.

"Hey, friend, love the outfit," Cordelia greeted, leaning close so her words could be heard over the raucous din and equally loud band. "Good night?"

Ione shifted and made herself comfortable. "Good tips. Easy to please clients for a shift that Arwen bequeathed to me. Nothing too crazy."

"That's great. You were a good sister to help out. Wish I could say the same about this. No idea where this crowd came from. One minute empty, and then poof. Packed." Cordelia turned, her black wig traveling with her. Like Ione, she had naturally dark blond hair, but Cordelia's went to the middle of her back. Ione had loose natural curls that remained hard to tame, so she chopped them right at her shoulder, keeping them long enough to pull back and tuck under a hat.

"Don't get me wrong, I'm not complaining," Cordelia said. "We need the revenue. Rent's going up January first."

"That sucks."

"Tell me about it. I'm hoping we don't have to close." Cordelia glanced down the bar and shouted, "I'll be right there" at a man who'd banged his mug with more force than necessary. She gave an annoyed shake of her head. "That's Barry. He's a regular. I should cut him off, but he lives on Second Street and walked here. Whatever you do, don't talk to him. If I have anything to say about it, he's going home alone." Cordelia shook a bloodred fingernail at the man. "If you do that again, Barry, I'm kicking you out!"

Ione glanced at her own short nails. "No worries on my end. Not my type. Make that never my type. Not in a million years my type."

Cordelia laughed. "No one is ever your type, because you're far too picky."

"I am not," Ione protested, knowing Cordelia spoke the truth. "And I prefer the word *selective*."

"Exactly, which is why I'm so impressed I made the cut."

"You always will," Ione said. She kept a small, tight circle. Friends since kindergarten, she and Cordelia had banded together after realizing they'd both been named after fictional characters, instead of being Emmas, Olivias or Isabellas, the top three names the year they'd been born. Cordelia was named after the character in *Buffy the Vampire Slayer*. And Ione's mother had named her after Hermione Granger from *Harry Potter and the Sorcerer's Stone*—the book, not the movie. Arwen's name came from *The Lord of the Rings*. Ione, already an outcast for being supersmart and socially awkward, had bonded with tomboy Cordelia for life.

"Besides, who else will put up with me?" Ione grinned.

"Now, you're being too hard on yourself. Time to get back on the horse and forget Henry, that jerk."

"Maybe if Will had a brother, I'd break my celibacy streak."

This time Cordelia did roll her eyes. "Please. One of him is enough of a handful, believe me. That's why I'm out here and he's manning the kitchen." Cordelia planted her hands on her hips, her engagement ring glittering as she watched Ione begin to dig into her pocket. "Don't even try to pay," Cordelia warned. "Owning this place has to have some perks for my best friend and future maid of honor. I will work out my financial issues."

"Fine," Ione conceded, securing her wallet. "But next time we go somewhere, I'm paying." She could afford small luxuries. The private consulting firm she worked for paid her handsomely and provided excellent benefits, including generous contributions toward retirement. Being single and on the road most of the time meant she saved most of her money, at least the portion she didn't use to pay her mom's medical bills. Thankfully, her mom's cancer was in remission.

"Tell you what, how about you give me a kick-ass bridal shower next spring in trade?" Cordelia suggested.

"Deal," Ione said, accepting the drink Cordelia was sliding toward her. She had to remember to request time off for that weekend and secure a full week's vacation in May for the wedding. She held the drink to the light. "What is this?"

"It's tonight's special. I call it Butterbeer Boo-tiful punch."

While she might have been named for the famous Muggle-born witch, it was Cordelia who loved all things *Harry Potter*. Ione studied the mug that contained an amber liquid topped with whipped cream. The cream sported gold sugar sprinkles and butterscotch swirls. She took a sip, blinked and held up the glass again. "Whoa. What is in here?"

"The punch is made from cream soda, seltzer and vanilla vodka. The topping is whipped cream mixed with brown sugar, vanilla and butter. Isn't it great? It's been so popular that we've had to make more than we expected."

"I can understand why. It's good. Different." Ione sipped again, the unique flavor growing on her.

"If you hate it, I'll grab you a beer or your standard white wine. Just let me know. By the way, some of our former high-school classmates are over by the band. Unless they've left." Cordelia turned and shook her finger. "Yes, Barry! I see you!" Cordelia moved to the other end of the bar, and called, "Don't make me set Will on you!"

Ione lifted her mug, slid off the stool and made her way toward the band. But she didn't see anyone she knew, even after circling the bar twice. She ignored the people who did a double take when they looked at her, something she'd done herself once or twice due to people's Halloween costumes.

After another sip of punch that made her glass half-empty, she jostled her way back toward the bar, often stopping short to allow others to pass. Parting the sea might be easier, she decided. Or perhaps creating a dam like the one she'd consulted on for a state park in Michigan. She fingered the purple felt hat to ensure it remained secured to her dark blond hair. Attempting to make her way again, she progressed a mere two feet when someone staggered backward. The movement clipped her arm as a person fell into her. "Hey!" she called.

But Ione's warning came too late as the contents of her glass sloshed. The liquid threatened to rise over the edge and splash outward, until a dark green shirtsleeve blocked the drunk. "Steady there," a deep male voice boomed through the noise as his fingers righted Ione's glass. The oblivious pirate stumbled toward the bathroom. "You okay? The drink didn't spill on you, did it?"

He was speaking to her. Ione turned toward the stranger. At five-eleven, she towered over many men, but with him she had to raise her eyes.

"Looks like nothing spilled on you." His voice was warm and deep, and his smile struck her like a lightning bolt. Her eyes widened. His dark hair swooped toward an eyebrow lifted in inquiry. His gray eyes narrowed in concern. He lifted his hand from her arm, and that stopped the tingles that were traveling to the tips of her toes, which were clad in black boots.

"You're not in costume." As the words slipped out, she clamped her mouth shut. Heat flamed across her cheeks. Was his aura so powerful it made her revert to her awkward teenage self? To the girl who'd never known what to say to boys?

"No, I'm not in costume." His deep, rich voice was like thick chocolate syrup running over vanilla ice cream. Decadent. Her body reacted to his obvious charms.

"I mean, you don't need a costume. You're fine just the way you are." *Oh, lord, that came out sounding even worse.* Mortified, she worked to extricate herself. "Thank you for saving my drink. For saving me. I appreciate your help." Ione squeaked out the last word before flinging a hand over her mouth to stop herself from saying anything more. Cordelia's brew must be stronger than she'd first thought if she'd turned into a babbling simpleton. Ione readied to step past him, but like salmon moving upstream, her way became blocked by a rapidly moving current of college-age kids maneuvering past. He took a step, diverting the flow to provide them more space.

"Thanks for the help. This place is packed."

"You're welcome." Dark hair fell dangerously low as his head tilted. "And as for a costume, I just came from a wedding. I guess I could have worn my tux, but I wanted to get out of it as soon as possible."

He was model-gorgeous. If he'd been in formal wear... Her mouth flooded with eager anticipation, as if he was a sugary sweet she was ready to eat. Cordelia might tease Ione about not having a type, but she did. *Him.* She'd make an exception for the man in front of her. Something about him triggered every one of her primitive urges, including desires that, if unchecked, threatened to make her act even more foolish. Her sexual response had her grasping for the first words she could find. "You didn't ditch your bride, did you?"

Good grief. That wasn't any better.

His face split into a smile the equivalent of 9.0 on the Richter scale, with dimples forming boomerang creases around his lips. "No. Just my family. My brother's fiancée sprang a surprise wedding ceremony on him, almost like an elopement but with everyone present. Needless to say, he and his wife are happily married and on their way to the honeymoon suite."

"And you're here. Alone." Her face flamed as the social awkwardness she'd worked so hard to eradicate returned with a vengeance. She'd never been someone who flirted, if that's what this was. Frankly, her responses to him were unknown and untried. It was as if some new persona had overtaken her.

"I'm alone." His gaze held hers a beat too long. Like a moth to a flame, she couldn't pull away. "I'd had enough of family. Wanted to get out." He glanced around, freeing her from some of his magnetism for at least a second or two. "This crowd's a bit young for me. But you're not."

"No." She stared at him, trying to comprehend the nonverbal messages reflected in those beautiful gray eyes. She was certain he was flirting with her. No. Wait. Maybe he was just being friendly. She'd misread cues before, especially as she understood animal mating far better than human courtships. Definitely one reason her relationship with Henry had tanked. She'd missed all the signs telling her he didn't want anything more than the physical.

She fixated on something the man in front of her said. "I'm also older than most everyone in here."

"When did college kids start looking twelve?"

"Cordelia has a strict ID policy," Ione said quickly. "Beaumont's serious about underage drinking."

His smile slipped and his eyebrows knitted together. "I'm not disbelieving you or trying to insult Cordelia, whoever she may be. I gave up college parties six years ago."

"Oh. Cordelia's the owner and my good friend. And got it."

His next words were as smooth as warm honey. "I like someone older and more experienced. They're much more interesting."

She sucked at understanding innuendo. She instead calculated the math. What he'd said about his age made him around twenty-eight. She was thirty-four. She had gotten her master's degree before he'd graduated high school. "Are you saying I'm old or interesting? Or both?"

He lifted his glass and stared at it a second too long, as if surprised to find the contents empty. Ione noticed a gaggle of young women appraising him like an iced cupcake. Ignoring them, he gestured. "I'm saying we should head to the bar, especially as that's where you were originally headed. Shall we?"

Since she was going there, anyway, she nodded. As a former college volleyball player, she was no shrinking violet. But he was broad-shouldered and fit, and people moved aside like Moses parting the Red Sea, allowing them to move through unimpeded. They soon found themselves at the bar, where, as if he'd manifested them, two barstools sat empty. Ione slid onto one and he took the other. "What are you having?" he asked.

Cordelia arrived, and as her friend's mouth opened, Ione gave a small shake of her head. Cordelia pointed at Ione's glass. "More brew?" Without waiting for an answer, Cordelia grabbed an empty glass. "Another two fingers?" This she directed at the man seated next to her.

He turned to Ione. "I'm either refilling or leaving. Is

it okay if I sit with you? I'd like to chat with you more. That is, if you agree. If not, I'm headed out. I don't want to drink alone, but I don't go where I'm not wanted."

Ione did a quick double take. He'd asked her permission to talk with her, which both shocked and surprised. "Sure. You can stay. I don't mind." Quite the opposite actually.

His presence meant she wouldn't drink alone, either, with no one to talk to but her friend, who was far too busy. Tonight, Ione would sit next to the most gorgeous man she'd ever seen. She hoped she managed not to run him off before it was time to leave. She'd always struggled with the interpersonal. She'd seen men's eyes glaze over, especially when they found her too brainy or something. She'd worked hard to improve her casual conversational skills.

"Excellent." In response to Cordelia's question, he held up two fingers to indicate he'd take another drink. "I'm glad."

Cordelia brought Ione a filled mug. She also sent Ione a glance that told her Cordelia would keep watch from behind the bar. Ione would be safe. Nothing would happen.

Unless Ione wanted it to.

As the man next to her directed that Oscar-winning smile in her direction, Ione decided the jury could remain out.

Chapter Two

As he lifted his first sip of Kentucky's best to his lips, Michael realized something fundamental. "You know," Michael said, "I don't even know your name."

And he wanted to know. He smoothed his brow so she didn't see his confusion. His reaction to her surprised him. He could tell she was pretty, despite her face paint. She sipped the whipped concoction and the gold-dusted cream clung to her upper lip. When her tongue gave the remnants a quick flick, Michael's libido groaned in unchecked response. He shifted to avoid embarrassing himself.

"It's Ione."

"Like the sea nymph." Unable to help himself, and wanting to test a theory, he offered his hand. She pressed her palm against his. Warmth fused their fingers and his skin heated. Yes, there was something here. He hadn't imagined it. "I'm Michael."

She gave him a curious smile. "Michael. Not Mike."

"Heck no. Or Mick or any other variation." He should release her hand, but touching her had sent another jolt through him. He'd never experienced this type of chemistry, and he was a man who'd been around enough to know the difference. "Just Michael."

"Michael seems formal. But not in a bad way. I have a feeling it suits you." Two of her fingers found the yellow-gold, custom-made signet ring he wore on his pinkie. She turned his hand to the light and he swore he saw fireworks. "Sort of like this. It's different."

These type of status symbols were common in his social circle. Her light touch made his nerves short-circuit, sending the type of devilish signals that always got him in trouble to his very receptive brain. "Gift from my parents when I graduated."

"It's nice."

He noted the black lace gloves she wore, which caused his interest to spike more than any jewelry had ever done.

She peered closer. "I was expecting a college class ring similar to what I have, but it's initials in a fancy script."

"My mom chose the design."

"I like it. It's different."

Keeping his hand fused to hers, he used his free hand to bring his glass to his lips. He needed the swallow of fiery bourbon to clear his head. She'd given him an opening to tell her that Stanford was the undergrad university of choice for the Clayton family. His and Edmund's MBAs had come from there, while Liam's was from Harvard in sustainable architecture. In his circle, credentials mattered, as did his bank account. But for some reason, he didn't want her to know who he was, especially as she clearly hadn't recognized him, even from the few articles in the Beaumont press. He wanted this chance to be himself, to be something other than the playboy women wanted to tame.

"Tell me more about the parents who gave you this," she said, finally severing their connection so she could sip her drink. His fingers missed her touch. "Do they live close by?"

Nope, she had no clue who he was. Relaxing, he sipped his whiskey and told her they'd moved to town a year or so ago.

"I grew up here," Ione said. "Born and raised. Then I left."

"Really? Tell me more." He wanted her to talk, to have a normal conversation that was more him listening than speaking.

Hours later, Michael concluded he'd chosen wisely by sitting with Ione. He hadn't laughed like this in ages. He'd stayed far longer in Kaiser's than he'd first planned. Despite the lure of the band playing one of this favorite songs, once he'd gone inside and seen the younger crowd, he'd almost turned around and left. But something had compelled him to stay, so he'd ordered a drink and wandered. He'd watched the band. Suffered the attentions of women six to seven years his junior, many with their enticing assets on full display in their sexy costumes.

He'd felt nothing whatsoever, until he'd met the woman currently sitting next to him. Ione was interesting and fresh. For one thing, she wore the least sexy costume of anyone in the room, which she'd explained was the uniform for leading the ghost tour he'd seen earlier. She'd told him about the Woman in White and he'd told her about visiting the Winchester Mystery House in San

Jose. She'd admitted no one had seen any ghosts tonight, minus the costumes worn by those out and about. He'd told her he hadn't felt anyone tugging on his shirt, which sometimes happened to visitors who went through the famed Winchester House.

"But that's to be expected," he said. "Ghosts aren't real."

She impulsively gave him a high five, the lacy texture of her glove tickling his palm. "Thank goodness someone else agrees. Of course, they're not. But it's good marketing and the ghost tour benefits the town."

"So you don't believe? Not even a tiny sliver?"

As if unable to help herself, Ione's face scrunched up and her nose wrinkled. He found her expression adorable. What was it about her?

"Of course, I don't. I'm into science, not pseudoscience. There are logical explanations for various phenomenon, like electromagnetic fields, or mold, or even carbon dioxide. And let's not forget the power of suggestion and good old human gullibility. Humans want to believe. They'll create meaning in their minds for purely psychological reasons. That's an entirely different field of study. Someone on my tour asked if one of the bats we saw could be Dracula." Ione took a sip of the night's special brew. "As if. He's a story, some gothic literature. Nothing more."

"It would make my life easier if he was real," Michael said. "Then I could put a stake through his heart and be done with him instead of having to deal with all his minions."

"What are you talking about?" She gave him a weird look, as if he'd grown horns. Perhaps he had.

"Bats," he told her. He paused, choosing his words carefully. Whenever he told women who he was, they more often than not saw dollar signs. Rachel, his last girlfriend, might have been an heiress, but even she'd wanted to be Mrs. Clayton after the first date. In hindsight, he should have made it their only date. Yet another failure on his part.

"I'm working on a project to develop a piece of old farmland and turn it into an eighteen-hole golf course out by the Beaumont Grand Hotel and the Beaumont Chateau. But when we were surveying the grounds, we discovered endangered gray bats on the property. They nest in a cave set into the bluff."

"What kind of bats? The scientific name," she prompted.

"Myotis grisescens." He'd used Google to learn the correct pronunciation and he'd practiced saying it.

"Really? They're rare." Her features had sharpened, showing her interest. Again, another point in her favor. "Most of their caves are south of the Missouri River, mainly in the Ozarks."

He was beyond impressed. "Yeah. The company I work for has one of the few caves with those bats that exist north of the river. Because of this, we can't develop along the bluff as we'd planned." He shook his head. "The CEO is not happy." His dad sure wasn't. They had to start building because they were hosting the PGA in three years.

Her hat didn't move as she shook her head. "No, you can't proceed. That would be illegal and against tons of federal wildlife codes, not to mention any state ones. *Myotis grisescens* is a protected species. But that's what makes it exciting."

Never had a Latin pronunciation sounded so sexy as it rolled off her tongue with ease. "I wouldn't describe it as exciting. It's stressful. For the last week, I've been trying to figure out what to do, since ultimately, the fate of the project rests on me. We have to build, but how?"

She fingered the handle of her mug. Half the contents remained. "How much land do you have?"

"I don't understand."

"If you don't have any land constraints, you could donate the land with the cave to the conservation department. You could set up a wildlife buffer, ensuring the bats would be not only be protected, but remain a part of your ecosystem. They help manage the insect population and eat the bugs that you don't want. You'd have to work with the appropriate government agencies to get that done, but it's doable. Donating the land might require your golf course to be redesigned, but since the bats are endangered, you can't build there, anyway."

She paused only long enough to draw a short breath. "Creating a buffer by donating land could be win-win and good PR. You could even sell bat-themed T-shirts once your course opens. But only if your client has enough land to be flexible. Otherwise, you'll need to figure out something to use it for besides a golf course." Even though her face paint was pale white, he caught a flush on her cheeks. "Sorry. I tend to ramble."

"I like it. My client has the land. It's a great idea and something to consider. Thanks."

She seemed both pleased and flustered by his compliment. "Well, that's what I do. I was working for a federal agency, but I wanted a change and I was tired of cold Alaska winters. Now I'm in private consulting.

I'm off to West Virginia on Monday to oversee a project the company I work for designed for a power plant."

He ignored the pang of disappointment. "You sound busy. Especially as you're also helping your sister out by being a tour guide." She'd told him that earlier.

She lifted the mug and drained the last of the night's specialty cocktail. "Exactly. Her husband is out of town and her regular guide got sick. So I stepped in and got to listen to people wondering if they'd find the Woman in White."

"Speaking of the Woman in White, what do you think of romance?" He followed the question by letting another sip of bourbon war its way through him. It was a personal question, so he tempered its delivery by adding, "I mean, the Woman in White is all about love. Would you pine after someone in the afterlife? If you believed in ghosts. Or were one." He checked his wince. So much for being smooth. He was as obvious as a teen trying to get his first date.

"That would mean I'd have to have someone in this life, so clearly I don't know." Michael filed that information away as she retrieved the glass of water the bartender had brought her. "I majored in wildlife conservation and management. In the animal kingdom, sex is mostly thought to be about propagation of the species. Nature doesn't expect everything to survive, and as far as we know, animals don't love each other like humans do."

"But what about those animals that seem to mourn? Sorry, I'm genuinely curious."

"It's fine. It's an area of scientific research and it interests me. The truth is, we don't have enough evidence to declare anything conclusively one way or the other. There is some research going on as to whether animals have sex for pleasure. A biologist at Mount Holyoke College, for instance, says that dolphins have sex all the time, including for social reasons. She studies dolphin clitorises and sexual activity." She sipped more water. "That feels like a weird thing to say, but science interests me. I could talk nonstop about it, but as my mom always said, it's not necessarily something anyone else wants to discuss."

"Don't be ashamed on my account. I don't mind. I'm finding what you say interesting. And seeking pleasure is nothing to be embarrassed about." Unless doing so made one tabloid fodder.

"We're humans and wired for it," Ione said.

"True. And I like the mystery. If humans had all the answers, life would be boring. I'm not making fun of you. I'm finding this conversation fascinating." He meant it. Normally his crowd discussed more trivial things, like fashion or the latest VIP hot spot. After a while, that was the same old same old and he was tired of it.

"I appreciate it. I have to try not to be so literal. It's one of my flaws."

"I prefer calling them quirks. And it would probably be better if I were more literal. But I like your ideas about the bats. I'm going to suggest donating the land with my company. See what they say. It might be the right solution." And he needed one, stat.

"I'm glad I could be of help." Even the black lipstick didn't diminish Ione's smile. "We need to work in harmony with nature, not against it. I wrote my thesis on that very subject. Well, that's the short version, anyway."

"Everything good over here?" The lead bartender—Cordelia—set down two more large glasses of ice water.

"Great," Ione said, then took a long sip of water. The movement allowed Michael to fixate on a neck a vampire would love to nibble. Michael averted his gaze before he found himself too tempted to join the undead. "So what sort of music do you like?" Ione asked, and thankfully the conversation went on.

They both liked alternative music and Italian food. They both liked taking vacations and had traveled widely. They both liked chocolate ice cream better than vanilla, and Ione's favorite Ted Drewes flavor was the original vanilla custard with hard shell topping spun through. New to the St. Louis area, Michael hadn't yet been to the landmark on Route 66, which Ione told him was a must-do activity.

Too bad she was leaving, or he might ask her out. On a warmer day they could lower the top on his Corvette, and she could show him some of the St. Louis landmarks he hadn't seen. But since she'd told him she was leaving, there was no point. Knowing their time was coming to an end, and since he wouldn't see her again, he found himself wanting to prolong the evening.

They'd both had enough alcohol to loosen their inhibitions without being too drunk for consent. That was a dangerous place—and Michael liked danger. He was wired differently from his brothers in that way. Edmund liked closing business deals and vanquishing the opposition. Liam loved conquering the mountain. Michael's sense of adventure lay in exploring the female form. But as of his move to Beaumont, he was trying to turn over a new leaf. He slid his hand farther away from hers, lest he be tempted to check if the desire between them hadn't been a fluke. The ice water sliding down his throat did little to cool the fire burning through him, but he tamped down the heat.

"So, Ione, you said you're heading to West Virginia for work?"

"Yes. I'll be gone for at least four months. My job ensures that projects comply with federal regulations protecting wildlife and natural resources. I'm working on renewable energy."

"My loss is their gain." He saluted her with his water glass. "What you do is impressive."

"It means I know a lot of acronyms and do work for the ESA, MBTA and BGEPA."

"You lost me. But whatever it means, don't sell yourself short. You clearly know more than me about a lot of things, like bats." Despite his degrees, she was probably a lot smarter than him, too. Unlike some, he didn't find the prospect intimidating. "You said you have a PhD?"

"I do. And those acronyms were the Endangered Species Act, Migratory Bird Treaty Act and Bald and Golden Eagle Protection Act. Basically, it means that I work with environmental permitting, assessment, and/ or compliance work. And now your eyes have glazed over and I've lost your attention."

"Not at all." He was even more fascinated. "You helped me with my company's bat problem, and for that I'm grateful. Also, one of my older brothers is into saving the planet, too." As part of his taking over as VP of the family wineries, Liam had insisted all Clayton Hotels be made as green as possible and carbon offsets purchased until each one of their hotels could be carbon-neutral. Michael was currently implementing those initiatives. "He's Mr. Nature."

"But not you."

Michael tossed his hands up and grinned. "Sadly, my idea of being outdoors is playing golf. I prefer my fun be indoors and my hotel experiences five-star. My brother? He'll rough it."

"But not you." From the way her lips pursed he could tell she wasn't impressed. Another point in her favor, making her different from most women he knew.

"There's nothing wrong with that, is there?" he asked.

She shook her head. "I never said I didn't like five stars. But even four are out my budget. Besides, I like camping. When I'm working in the woods, I'm usually staying in a tent. Carry in and carry out. I don't mind roughing it. It's often necessary, given the remote places I work." She checked her phone. He had the same time on his watch: almost midnight. "I should go."

He could prolong their encounter no longer, a foreign, bittersweet feeling. "It's been nice meeting you, Ione. I live down the block, so I'll walk you out as far as the curb. If you're okay with that."

She signaled her agreement. He placed several twenties on the bar, enough to cover their drinks, and waited while she gathered her things.

The band was on its last set, meaning the crowd had thinned. They reached the door with no mishaps and stepped out into a blast of cold. He shivered. Perhaps the Woman in White was real, because it certainly felt as if something had passed through him. The chill seeped into his bones.

"You didn't check the weather report, did you?" Ione adjusted the collar of her coat to block out the wind.

He pointed south. "I don't live far. I won't freeze. No need to worry."

"Well, my car's parked behind the inn, so I'll walk with you. You seem safe enough."

"Thanks, I think." He'd never been thought of as safe before. The internet trolls had called him unreliable. Dangerous. A heartbreaker. Or worse, a Darth Vader who destroyed women like Vader destroyed Alderaan, completely and without remorse.

"I mean it as a compliment," she said. Mere inches from staring him eye to eye, Ione fell into step beside him, easily matching his stride. "Haven't you heard about that question where if a woman walks alone in the woods, would she rather meet a man or a bear? Everyone picks the bear. Well, I've met several bears, and after working with a bunch of chauvinists, I agree with the women who choose the bear. Bears I can handle. I've learned to handle the chauvinists, too. You seem okay. I'm not wrong, am I?"

Passing under the glow of the streetlamp, Michael kept his hands firmly in his pockets and his gaze forward. "No, you're not. I'm all about consent. Willing parties. That sort of thing."

Ione tossed him another sideways glance, one he caught from the corner of his eye. "With your looks, you probably find a lot of willing women. I'm sure they throw themselves at you. Is that why you asked me about romance earlier? It made me wonder if you were hitting on me. I should have asked you before."

Michael found himself surprised. "I must be losing

my touch if you didn't know I'm interested. I'd ask if I could see you again, but you're leaving. I thought it might be rude to assume anything, especially as I'll be here and you'll be in West Virginia. I'm not asking you to go home with me. Unless you want to go home with me."

Minus their footsteps, silence fell as Ione absorbed that. North Main turned into South as they made their way along the sidewalk. Once they parted in front of the inn, she'd leave this crazy night behind. "What do you mean?" she asked. "Are you being serious about me going home with you? Because of the way my brain works, I need things spelled out. Were you joking?"

"While I was trying to lighten the moment, I wasn't joking. I find you very desirable."

Pleasure raced through her, only to war with doubt, because Henry had sowed the seeds of her insecurities deep. "Really? Why? I find that odd because I'm dressed like this."

His tiny shrug emphasized broad shoulders that were the perfect width to rest her head against. "Chemistry? A connection? I can't be more specific."

"Huh," she said as she considered his words. Having a man as gorgeous as he was speak to her so freely was new and different. "You need to know I'm not good with subtleties. And while your words don't feel out of the blue after our conversations tonight, this does feel odd."

His eyebrows knitted together. "How so? We're consenting adults. We can do whatever we want."

"Yes, but…" She faltered and stopped walking. Had there been a time she did whatever she wanted? Besides eating an extra piece of chocolate. "You have to know how attractive you are."

"Yes. And?"

Ione gestured to her face. "I'm obviously not your usual type. I'm not as attractive as some of the women in the bar. I saw them looking at you."

His frown didn't lessen and nerves consumed her. "You're making me sound like I'm slumming by being with you. Let me reassure you that I'm not. I've never stood on vanity. I want you because you're you, and that's about as clear as I can make it."

As Ione absorbed his words, Michael checked his frustration. It wasn't Ione's fault. "I'm sorry. I'm a little touchy about this."

How many times had Edmund and Liam teased Michael about his looks or the fact women flocked to him like flies to honey? Not that his brothers were ugly. But Michael had been a woman magnet since birth. He didn't want Ione to see him that way. "Being desired is tiring. Do they see me? Or just a face? Maybe I want to shed that persona. Like a cicada sheds its shell."

A black-stained mouth he still longed to kiss dropped open in confusion. "You want to shed your nymphal exoskeleton?"

"Is that what they're called?" He shoved his hands deeper into his front pockets and remembered she'd asked him to be direct. "I apologize for the odd metaphor. And I don't know anything about their life cycle except for the fact that those empty shells were all over the place last year and that they flew around screeching and dive-bombing everyone. It was annoying. Which you are not."

The grounds crews at various properties had also had to sweep away the shells twice a day. Thankfully, they didn't have to deal with that again for over a decade. "And they were loud." He was blowing this. He should get her number and go home.

"They are loud. Males can reach a hundred decibels with their mating calls. But at least those two broods won't emerge at the same time again until 2245. I don't believe either of us will be around to see that. And as inconvenient as they are, cicadas play a vital ecological role, providing food sources for animals and enriching the soil." Her hand went over her mouth, an unconscious gesture. "Sorry, I'm being scientific again."

He liked that about her, but assumed from her sour expression that others didn't. He found her a fresh change from women who wanted to discuss nothing but fashion or gossip about people they knew.

"I don't mind. You spoke like a true biologist. What you do impresses me. You impress me. If not, I wouldn't have kept talking with you. I certainly don't pity you, and despite what I said earlier, I can drink alone. I find you interesting and I enjoyed getting to know you."

"Understood." Her one little nod sent a jolt through him.

"Talking with you was a pleasurable way to pass the time. I enjoyed it. You're brilliant. Unjaded. Keep being you because I like it." He moved forward to shake her hand. "Good luck in West Virginia. It was nice to meet you, Ione."

She took his hand in a firm grip. "Same, Michael."

The way his name rolled off her tongue attracted him further. Too bad she was leaving. The corner of her lip twitched as if she'd made a split-second deliberation. "I do have a question before we part."

"Ask away." As long as he could keep holding her hand, he'd give her anything she wanted.

"Would I be one of those forward woman whom I saw giving you side glances if I said I don't want the evening to end? That I want a few more hours of your time?"

Was she being serious? Michael stared at her for a long moment. Would he regret this opportunity if he passed? He decided he would. Turning over a new leaf could wait until tomorrow.

As the words propositioning Michael left her lips, Ione chose not to recall them, despite his staring at her strangely. Shockingly, she'd meant them. Never had she been this forward.

Her request, though, hadn't come from any residual alcohol that might be running through her bloodstream. Her proposition didn't even come from a desire to wipe the slate clean. To end her post-Henry Summers, self-imposed celibacy, she needed to have sex again at some point, sort of like the concept of falling off a horse and getting back on. Or in scientific terms, fail in one hypothesis, create a new one and try the experiment again.

She'd acted on pure impulse. Maybe it was the fact that Michael was the perfect, prime male specimen to prove Henry's theory of Ione's deficiencies wrong. Her ex had declared her bad at sex. Was she as terrible as he said? She'd never know unless she had sex again. Michael seemed to want her, so logic said he'd make an excellent test subject. She'd noticed the lustful glances the younger women had sent in his direction that night. In the laws of nature, he was the fittest. In her field of the animal kingdom, he'd be described as the powerful male the female of the species wanted for her mate, fulfilling that innate biological quest for copulating with the gene pool's best. In scientific terms, the desire she was feeling toward him was elemental and natural. But why did he want her when he had so many others to choose from? She was no beauty queen, no ten out of ten. She was nerdy and enjoyed putting on river waders and studying crayfish. Or crawling on her stomach into a cave to survey bat guano.

A man like Michael was not in her league. But for some reason he wanted her. And she wasn't looking for anything long-term, especially as she was headed to West Virginia to work on a project that would add hydropower capacity to multiple dams along the Ohio River. She'd be responsible for ensuring the projects didn't impede river flow or harm wildlife, and that they met all federal and state guidelines.

"I don't want the night to end, either, but let's be clear on what you're suggesting," Michael said. "Like you, I want things spelled out."

Ione liked that about him. Not only did he ask her permission, but he also didn't make any assumptions. "That's fair. I could want to go to late-night dinner or something. But I don't. I want sex. One night is all I want or can promise, so I figure being direct is best. That's my nature, anyway."

"One night freely given because you're leaving," Michael clarified.

"Yes. Exactly. I'm hoping I'm reading the situation correctly as I'm not good at doing so, but I agree there's a sexual current flowing between us. Pheromones are making my body respond to yours. I'd like to take advantage of that chemistry you mentioned, see if we can enjoy some mutual pleasure."

"I don't think I've ever had such a proposition."

She plastered on a benign expression, the one designed to hide any pain, the one she'd perfected by being a female in a man's world. "You can ignore my proposition if you'd like. I'm not some animal in heat." Mortification spread through her, triggering even more insecurities, as she realized how crass her words might have sounded, a fact confirmed when Michael peered at her curiously.

"I prefer the term *lovemaking*."

"But is it really love?" She retrieved her car fob from her pocket. Of course, he would reject her. She'd made a mess of things. She was tall and gangly and dressed like she'd come from the graveyard, which she essentially had. Even when scrubbed clean, Henry had described her as a six that improved to an eight if one drank a six-pack of five-percent beer. She began to turn, but stopped when Michael placed his hand on her forearm.

The streetlight cast shadows over his face, showcasing angular cheekbones and a perfect nose. His DNA should be studied and catalogued. "Where are you going? I didn't say no. In fact, I'm one-hundred-percent ready to test a hypothesis of my own."

"Oh? You have a hypothesis?"

He toyed with her fingers, creating little shivers that traveled along her spine. "I can't say how scientific it will be, especially as science classes and I were never friends, but touching you is doing things to me, too. I'd like to test just how compatible we'll be once you're in my bed."

His words thrilled, as if the ground she stood on tilted, and not because of the cobblestones beneath their feet. They were going to do this. "Okay. As long as I can wash my face before you kiss me. You will kiss me, won't you?" Kissing didn't matter to have sex, and Henry hadn't liked it. But for some reason, tonight kissing seemed important. If she was going to put herself into the care of a handsome man, she wanted the full experience.

He took her other hand in his and Ione swore parts of her melted. "Why wait? Why not take a taste now, be sure this is what you want, a theory you want to explore. All you have to do is say yes, and I'll start the experiment."

"Yes." The word burst forth, and liking how he'd described their potential coupling in scientific terms, Ione lifted her face to his. The moment his lips met hers, she swore fireworks erupted. She suspected he had "accomplished kisser" hardwired into his DNA, but as a powerful sensation worked like river rapids and swept her away, Ione didn't care about his genetic code. Instead, all rational thought was tossed aside. Surely even someone as well-versed in biological science as she was could let passion rule every now and then, let it sweep her away.

She missed his lips the moment he lifted them from hers. He caught her gaze. "Well?"

The sample had whet her appetite to continue the exploration. She used the back of her thumb to rub some of her black lipstick from his lips. She liked his cockiness, the innate self-assurance of a man who knew exactly who he was. He was the universe's gift to women, and for one night, that gift belonged to her. Cordelia would approve, tell Ione to break her self-imposed rules. And no one's kisses had ever made her so wanton or ready to engage.

"I'd say my place or yours, but I'm staying with my sister," she told him.

"My apartment's right there." He pointed.

She gave him what she prayed was the sexiest smile she could manage. "Then yours."

She left her hand resting in his as they walked south, keeping her palm there more to reassure herself she'd made the correct choice than to worry he'd change his mind and flee. He unlocked a door on the side of the building and she followed him upstairs. "Bathroom is down the hall. What do you want to drink?"

Now that she stood in his apartment, she wanted her complete wits about her. She suspected he'd had many lovers and knew the score of a one-night stand far better than she did, especially considering she'd never had one.

"Water's fine," she called as she left him standing in the living room. She'd never been in this space before, but knew several people who'd previously rented the apartment, like Shelby's husband, Luke. Ione stepped into the hall bath, finding it stocked with everything she'd need to scrub her face. That gave her pause, thinking how many other women might have come here before her, but she chose to ignore the doubts that arose. She didn't own him. She had no claim. They weren't geese mating for life. She could have her first one-night stand. See what the fuss was about.

She took off the purple hat and fluffed out the dark blond hair she'd thankfully washed that morning. She removed her coat and scarf, then folded them over the edge of a sparkling clean bathtub. She shed her sweatshirt, stripping down to the cami top she had on underneath. She hesitated, then kicked off her boots and began to unbutton her jeans. She rinsed off, and with a face devoid of makeup and her curly hair loose to her shoulders, she walked barefoot out into the living room in nothing but her underwear.

"Wow." Gray eyes widened in male appreciation that even she could recognize. He held two bottles of water and handed her one.

"I figured getting almost naked would save time, be more practical." Ione refused to fold her arms over her chest and instead broke the seal on the bottle.

"And you're always practical."

"Mostly. My mind is extremely linear." She let the cold water run down her throat. Either he had the heat on, or she was already on fire, because she was warm and toasty while standing in nothing but her black camisole top and matching panties.

She wasn't ashamed of her athletic and toned body. From sports to working outdoors, she'd kept her shape. She had plenty of misgivings and insecurities to keep her awake at night, but being naked wasn't one of them. She set the water bottle on the counter. "I've propositioned you, so I wanted you to see I was serious. I don't play games. Unless they're volleyball or *Monopoly*."

"I'm very good at owning hotels." He fingered a black

strap. She reminded him of a sea nymph come to life from the artwork his parents had donated to the Portland Art Museum. "I like this. So, Ione, beautiful sea nymph, what's my role in this? If my apartment is your science lab, what is it you want me to do?"

She considered. Grew bold. "Whatever I tell you." She almost faltered. Henry had called her the most unadventurous and boring lover he'd ever had. She might have managed Henry's deliberate dent to her pride had he not announced his review of her sexual performance to everyone within earshot, including calling her frigid. Tonight she wanted to be fearless. Take charge.

"Tell me. What it is that you want me to do?" Michael's tone was notably huskier than before.

"First, I want to do this." She circled him, her fingers tracing his back and abdomen. He made to kiss her, but she put a finger on his lips. He nipped at it. "And this." Both her hands undid the button at his waist. He shoved pants and boxers down and kicked all clothing aside, freeing his lower half. "And this."

She grabbed the hem of the green Henley, and up and over went his shirt until he stood in his birthday suit. She circled again, tracing a finger along the curve of his lower back before rounding to the front. He made no attempt to hide himself. Why would he? He was built like Michelangelo's *David*, but bigger. Thicker. Better. Even more handsome. Men like Michael were as rare as a two-headed snake. They existed, but were not seen often. Michael was perfection; she was the awkward one. She bit her lip but refused to chicken out now that she'd come this far. She could do this. Be in control and give herself this moment. "You can touch yourself."

A dark eyebrow arched in query. "Is that a request?"

"Yes." She watched as he took himself in his palm. He slid his hand over his shaft. Made the motion again.

She lifted her gaze to find his locked on her. "Do you like that?" he asked. She bit her lip and nodded. "What do you want me to do next? Your wish is my command."

Ione was in over her head, like that one time she'd jumped off a bridge and it had taken her extra seconds to surface. She might have told him he had to do whatever she instructed, but she was an inexperienced dancer on an unfamiliar stage. Time to yield the lead to a skilled partner. "Take me to bed."

He swept her into his arms and cradled her to his lightly hair-dusted chest. "And once you're there?"

Surprised he'd lifted her so easily, she cupped a chin covered with delicious light stubble. "Show me everything."

"That I can do. And will." He brought his lips to hers, the kiss sending Ione spiraling. He lowered her to the bed as if she was a feather, and with a skillful touch, slid her underwear over her legs until they disappeared over his shoulder. He lowered his mouth to her core.

Ione clutched the bedcovers as the magic began. He nipped. Tongued. Tasted the place between her thighs. Took her to heights before unobtainable. As her shuddering orgasm subsided, he kissed his way up her stomach, sliding hands and mouth over breasts straining for attention. Her top disappeared. Experienced fingers went lower, moving into her heat and sliding in and out. His actions made her body shake again with pleasure, and before she came again, he lifted his head. He grinned with primal male satisfaction. "Like that? Is that what you wanted?"

"Yes. But more." She'd never felt these things before, and the words whooshed out as a multitude of nerve endings demanded even greater release. While this might be just sex, and while she knew there was a reasonable scientific explanation for the pleasure she was experiencing, tonight seemed different. Like it was somehow more. As if she'd undergone a metamorphosis. He was a master artist, and she was a paintbrush under his intuitive touch.

"Give me everything."

"Everything?" He nuzzled her neck. His heated exhale sent delicious little quivers racing to the blue-painted toenails she curled into the comforter.

"Everything," she repeated before capturing his roving head and returning his lips to hers for another long, passionate kiss. She broke off, pressing her feverish cheek to his. "I want it all. Show me."

He captured her mouth again and lowered his hand, his fingers dancing over her until she could bear no more. Even his opening the condom wrapper was seduction. The moment slowed, the act deliberate and natural—nothing forced. Nothing awkward. Nothing but passion waiting to be unleashed into pure pleasure. His gaze never left hers. She was with him at first thrust and the next, her satisfaction mirroring his.

She floated. She flew. Their joining went beyond the basics of biology. Her mind registered the seismic shift, that moment when their smiles disappeared and the sex became something more, something transcendent. Could she call it lovemaking, the word he'd used earlier? Whatever it was, a sacred form of sexual intensity took over and Ione let her body have the gratification being with Michael created. Her motives switched from a drive to erase whatever failures had come before to something she couldn't describe. The pleasure she found was like going from crawling to walking and suddenly discovering she could run. Like she'd opened a portal to an uncharted dimension and transformed into a willing, wanton woman, one who pleased the man she was with while enjoying herself.

Tonight was evolution. Not a reset, but a new path. She held him close as they both recovered from their respective orgasms. He kissed the tip of her nose. "Stay the night. Don't go. I'll be back."

She threw an arm over her forehead to block the light flickering to life in the en suite bathroom. He shut the door and she glanced around. She should find her clothes. At least be covered when he returned. Wasn't that what happened in the movies? Wasn't this how she was supposed to act? She didn't know.

Minus a college boyfriend, she'd never spent a full night with a man. Henry had liked having his own space, and since her apartment had been right down the hall in the same complex, they'd had sex and she'd walked home and slept alone. Stay with Michael? The thought caused a spike of fear. Would he find her lacking? Would it make her feel things for him she shouldn't?

But before she could find her clothes and flee, he was stepping out of the bathroom, the light flickering off and the darkness concealing them as he slid under the covers and reached for her. His arms spooned her to his chest, and he snuggled his chin into the curve of her neck. "Are we going to sleep?" she asked.

His lips found her flesh and nipped gently. His palms found her breasts. "Eventually. Until then, I'm giving you everything you asked for, and more."

Chapter Three

Spring was Michael's favorite season. Too bad he wasn't outside to enjoy the beautiful mid-May day. That might have at least helped with his current foul mood, especially following a long, brutal and gloomy winter that had extended into late April. However, instead of sitting on a warm, white sandy beach somewhere, he sat on a leather chair placed at the head of a smooth, mahogany conference table facing his father. And today, Michael simply wasn't in the mood. Hadn't been since that night with Ione.

The irony of being inside four claustrophobic walls didn't escape him, nor did the fact he hadn't been himself since that night. Maybe that's why he fixated on the weather, and that the one thing he'd looked forward to when relocating to Beaumont was that the St. Louis area had two hundred days of sun, give or take, compared to Portland's one hundred and fifty or so.

It had been a rough spring. The St. Louis region had received so much rain that both the Missouri and Mississippi Rivers had already flooded and crested once. Thankfully, only the floodplains had been inundated, but the constant rain had meant little foot traffic for local businesses. Today, the sun had chosen to finally show, and he wanted to be outside on a restaurant patio. Or at the area wineries. Something. Anything.

He was tired of the Midwestern gray gloom that had lingered long past the official start of spring. He'd also discovered why Missourians often described their daily forecast as going from one extreme to another in a matter of hours. Ever since Halloween, he'd experienced the massive heat-to-cold swings in temperature, and vice versa, multiple times. It was like being on a pendulum that constantly went from one side to the other. The weather mirrored his life and the woman he couldn't get out of his head. He didn't regret his night with her. Quite the opposite. Their lovemaking had been perfect, both mentally and physically. It had been more than sex for sex's sake. That night had been a calm in the storm, a rare moment of peace. They'd parted with no drama and no scandal followed in her wake. Just a residual desire he had to vanquish at some point. Even if the next time didn't live up to the memory, he wanted to see her again.

Was that why he hadn't walked away from his job once the year he and Liam had promised their father had been completed? Work kept him from thinking of Ione and the one night he couldn't forget.

"How are we going to solve this latest problem?" Michael's father asked from the other end of the table, his gray-eyed gaze firmly on his son.

Refusing to squirm under the direct scrutiny that often found him lacking, Michael stilled his fingers and stopped twisting the pen he'd been holding. "I'm working on it," he said. "You know I just got back."

For the past two weeks, he'd been visiting Clayton

Hotels around the world, something Edmund used to do before he'd met Lana. Even with flying in comfort on the company jet, Michael wasn't over the jetlag. "Lest you forget, I was in Australia and New Zealand. And before I came here, I dealt with the problems in Memphis from when the levee broke. I'm doing my job. You tapped me to do a job and I'm doing it. *Still* doing it. And I'm sorry to snap, but you need to show some grace. I'm doing what you asked."

His dad's mouth opened and shut before forming a thin line. Michael knew his father had bitten back a comparison of Michael to his older brother Edmund, who so far had shown no inclination to resume his traditional corporate role. After twelve months doing half his brother's former job, Michael understood why. If Ione had asked him to go with her that morning, Michael would have flown the coop, too.

"We promised the people of Beaumont we'd continue to create jobs." His father continued to press his point. "With our properties running at capacity, we're ready for the next phase."

"Yes, I know." Michael dropped the pen to the table, and it rattled on the wood with a tiny click. "We have a waiting list to stay at the Chateau and the Grand is above targeted occupancy. I can't help that we've encountered unexpected environmental problems on the next phase."

"No, but you haven't solved them, either. We're behind schedule on building the next hotel and eighteen holes," his father replied. "Surely, you should have found a solution by now? That's your job."

Michael laced his fingers together. "We also promised the people of Beaumont we would be strategic in our construction. Unlike some of the newer projects in the county that stripped everything bare first, we've worked with the environment, not against it. That means dealing with this latest hiccup in a socially responsible manner. You know our adherence to that model is why Liam has agreed to return for another year. You can take comfort in the fact that the hotel is ready to break ground. That's on schedule."

"No one will visit a golf course resort if there's no golf course." Michael's dad's lips remained in a thin line. Michael checked his groan and wished Liam was here to help run interference. But Liam and his wife and their five-month-old twins were in Nepal, laying the groundwork for the creation of a new school.

His father frowned. "As for the county, I never said we were going to clear-cut trees or bulldoze the topsoil. But progress comes with some sacrifice and the town needs to understand that. Clayton Holdings sacrificed when we donated the land where the cave is to the Department of Conservation so we could save some silly bats. Now, we're having to sacrifice for what, some birds?"

"They were endangered gray bats. A rare species. And they aren't just *some birds*. They're bald eagles. America's national symbol." His dad's gaze narrowed as he judged Michael's exasperated tone. "We need to do the right thing, like we did with the bats."

How they'd dealt with the bats was something Michael was proud of. After Ione had given him the idea to donate the land, Michael had learned that twenty percent of the total population of this species of endangered bats lived in Missouri, and between white noise syndrome and pesticides, the bats needed saving. What would she think of Clayton Holdings finding an active eagles' nest? He had no way of knowing, because even though they'd talked until the wee hours of the morning in between multiple bouts of lovemaking, they hadn't exchanged contact information. In hindsight, he regretted that omission. It still rankled that the first time he'd spent an entire night with a one-night stand she'd walked away without a backward glance. Eva would say turnabout was fair play, not that Michael had told his sister anything about what he'd done after he'd left Liam's wedding reception.

"We'll figure out what to do about the eagles, but you need to remember they're a protected species," he told his dad.

"I don't care. There has to be a way to move them," his father said, refocusing Michael's attention to the matter at hand. "We had to shift where we could build because of the bats, and because of that, what should have taken weeks has taken months. I hate being behind schedule. When are we seeing the final plans?"

"I hope by next week. The Good-4 Environmental consultant arrives today. It's a new person as the one we used last time is on paternity leave. And as for those bats, you should at least acknowledge we got a lot of good PR out of donating the acreage."

Too bad Eva wasn't here to help calm his father. Eva simply had a way with him that Michael didn't, perhaps because she was the baby of the family and the only girl. Thankfully, his siblings had supported Michael's idea of protecting the bats through land donation. That had made it easier to convince their father. "We did the right thing," Michael emphasized.

"It was one of your better ideas," his father admitted, offering rare praise. "But that still doesn't solve our current problem. We're hosting Beaumont's PGA tournament in a few years and we need to break ground on the golf course or we're not going to be able to meet our commitment to the contracts we signed. Damn birds." His father pounded his fist on the table. "At least the hotel should be on track."

What would Ione say about his latest problem, especially since Clayton Holdings couldn't afford to donate any more land? When the surveyors and architects had rendered the new plans for another Chateau-sized hotel and the accompanying eighteen-hole golf course built on former farmland, everything had gone according to schedule. Building permits had been issued. Sites readied, until workers had discovered an active eagle nest with two adult birds and two nestlings, and everything had once again ground to a halt.

One upside to the shutdown was that Clayton Holdings had set up a livestream so everyone could watch the nest's occupants. Since Beaumont County had fewer than five total eagle nests, that action had earned immeasurable goodwill. The downside—another delay.

Since eagles were federally protected, Michael's environmental team would be dealing with the US Fish and Wildlife Service and the Missouri Department of Conservation again.

Because of this, Clayton Holdings had hired Good-4 Environmental to help navigate the company's next steps. Liam's preferred consulting firm would also work on Liam's pet project—building pollinator habitats at the hotels and wineries. The rep, though, hadn't been anyone Liam knew, but Michael's brother had reassured him that anyone Good-4 sent would be good.

Ten minutes before his meeting with his father, Michael had received an email that Good-4's Dr. Hermione Scott would arrive later this afternoon. An executive-level administrative assistant had reserved her a minisuite at the Beaumont Grand, which was the closest hotel to both project sites. As long as the problem was solved quickly, Michael thought the cost well worth it. He'd also authorized the company plane to retrieve her from Atlanta.

"The consultant is on her way. Once we have a plan, I don't expect any more delays." Michael resisted crossing his fingers for good luck, especially when his father made what sounded like a disbelieving harrumph.

Michael worked to appease his father, as he had since his earliest memory. "It's the same firm Liam used when he built his house in Colorado, and the same one we used for the bats. The new hotel will be using solar and geothermal power, as will the clubhouse expansion at our current eighteen-hole course. Having someone ensuring we're in environmental compliance with the law will make things go smoother and faster. Liam also wants pollinator habitats at our American vineyards in order to support the viability of our grape vines. This consulting firm was working on that already, so we're simply adding to the scope of our contract."

"Nothing else better arise," Michael's dad said. "I want to step down, but this is why I—"

"I understand. You've made your point clear."

"Good." His dad seemed satisfied, and while Michael wanted to say "it's nature, Dad," he wisely kept his mouth shut so that the meeting ended. It had gone on long enough.

After his father left, Michael swiped open the live feed and watched the baby eaglets sleep. They would leave the nest somewhere around ten to twelve weeks after hatching. That would be the start of July.

Hopefully they'd find a solution, the project would get underway and his father would be happy. Then Michael, who hadn't slept with anyone since Ione and who found himself more and more at loose ends every day—even with his new girlfriend of a month who kept asking why he wasn't interested in sex—could finally figure out exactly what he wanted to do with his life. If Edmund and Liam could find happiness, so could he.

As the private jet winged its way toward Beaumont, Ione gripped the plush armrest with more force than necessary. The plane ride had been smooth the entire way, thanks to the pilot, whom she'd met briefly, so her actions were based more on fear of the unknown rather than any turbulence.

"Would you like anything else, Dr. Scott?" The flight attendant stood there, a pleasant smile on her face. "Chris said we'll be landing in about an hour."

"I'm good, thank you," Ione said, even though she was far from it. She was on the Clayton Holdings jet, as in *Michael Clayton*.

Michael, the man she'd slept with Halloween weekend. Michael, the Portland Playboy of world renown. As part of her due diligence, Ione always did an internet search on her clients. She'd started with Edmund Clayton before moving to his son, Edmund the Third. She'd researched Liam, whose pollinator restoration had already been in her firm's pipeline, a project she'd implement.

When she'd noticed the date of Liam's wedding, something had tickled the neurons in her prefrontal cortex, creating an awareness of sorts as buried memories returned. Long before Ione had joined Good-4 Environmental, her bosses had done work for Liam. The project she'd been assigned was an eagles' nest that had been found on land for the newest Clayton hotel and eighteen-hole golf course. When she'd read the words *golf course*, the hairs on Ione's arms had stood at attention. She'd found an article on Clayton Holdings donating land to save bats, and alarm bells had screamed when she'd seen Michael's photo. She should pay more attention to her own firm's doings, but the company did have five nationwide offices. She simply couldn't keep track of all the projects.

She never would have taken this assignment had she known. Okay, that was wishful thinking. The reality was that she was the only consultant whose latest project had finished, making her immediately available. She had also wanted to go home. She was needed in Beaumont by a sister now going through a divorce, a mother whose cancer had suddenly returned two months ago and a best friend who was in danger of losing the bar she loved while trying to plan for her May wedding.

Ione didn't believe in fate or the universe pulling strings, but if such things existed, the stars had aligned to bring her back to Beaumont. As for Michael, he'd been pictured with a stunning brunette last week, so he'd clearly moved on. Why wouldn't he? He was handsome, rich and the VP in charge of the hotel division, second only to his father, who was CEO. He was too far up the food chain to notice her.

Best-case scenario, if she did see him, she'd pretend nothing had happened. Surely, he would follow her lead.

She took one final sip of water and gave the empty glass to the flight attendant. Ione had been in private planes before, especially as that was how one reached remote areas of Alaska, but the luxury of this jet put those single-engine Cessnas to shame. Clearly, the necessity of getting her to Beaumont and dealing with the various federal and state agencies outweighed curbing carbon-dioxide emissions. When calculated per passenger, flying commercial and taking public transportation was far better for the planet.

The plane coasted to a stop on the tarmac, and Ione found an SUV idling nearby. The driver loaded her luggage into the back. With the days getting longer, Ione had arrived just before dark and the last vestiges of the sun peeked over the horizon, creating a soft orange glow as the car made the forty-five-minute trek to Beaumont. She texted her sister she'd arrived in town. Arwen would let their mother know—their mom had moved in with Arwen because the aggressive chemo treatments had made her too weak to live on her own. The family home had been sold, with little left after the first and second mortgages had been paid off.

Ione felt guilty. She hadn't known Arwen's marriage had been on the rocks Halloween weekend. She should have asked. Having his mother-in-law move in two months ago had been too much for Arwen's husband, and he'd moved in with his parents. Ione hadn't liked John, but she'd tolerated him for her sister's sake. No longer. Ione glanced at the return text. Arwen told her their mother was sleeping and it would be better if Ione visited sometime tomorrow. She would, after her meetings with the Clayton Holdings representatives. Ione liked the message and waited as the driver parked under the portico of the Beaumont Grand.

Within seconds, a bellman whisked away her suitcases, a packed tent and the steel cases containing her camping equipment and various scientific tools. In West Virginia, when she'd gotten a few days off, she'd hiked and camped solo in the Appalachian Mountains. Ione shifted the backpack onto her shoulder, but before she could approach the front desk, a woman wearing a white blouse, blue pencil skirt and low heels came forward. "Dr. Scott? I'm Lucinda, one of the assistant managers. How was your trip? We're delighted you've arrived safely. I've got your room keys here. While you're staying with us, Mr. Clayton said you aren't to worry about a thing. In fact, I've arranged for a complimentary spa visit for whenever you'd like. I've left the details in your suite."

"Thank you. That's kind." And unnecessary. But since they had, maybe she would indulge.

"Do you need any additional help?" Lucinda asked. "There was a small hiccup with your rental car, but we've put a UTV at your disposal until it arrives so you can at least see the property. If you have dinner in the bar or restaurant tonight, charge the meal to your room and we'll take care of your bill."

"Thank you. I appreciate it. I'm good." Ione noted

the room number and made her way to the elevators. Ione's fifth floor "mini" suite was larger than her Atlanta apartment and consisted of a luxuriously furnished living room, a stylish bedroom with a king-size bed and a huge bathroom with a walk-in shower and separate bathtub. Well, Michael had said that he liked his hotels five-star. If this was a small suite, what did the penthouses look like? Or the fancier Beaumont Chateau a little bit farther down the road? Or the soon-to-be-built resort hotel? She couldn't imagine.

She removed the luggage rack from the closet and set her suitcase atop the leather straps. She'd learned long ago never to use the dresser drawers in a hotel, especially after leaving some of her cargo shorts inside a drawer and not discovering the loss until she was thousands of miles away. She did hang some things in the closet and left the door open to remind herself they were there. She unpacked her toiletries and paced the hotel room. She texted Cordelia to let her know she was in town and received a return text saying she was at the bar and that she should come visit. Ione had eaten before she left, but that didn't matter. She had to tell Cordelia about Michael. As her nerves flared, she sent an "on her way" and called for a ride. Time to head to downtown Beaumont. There was a certain person she wanted to see.

Michael hadn't been in Kaiser's since the night he'd met Ione, but for some reason that's exactly where he found himself tonight, even sitting on the same barstool. The only difference was that instead of a band, the St. Louis Cardinals baseball game played on the TVs located high in the corners of the bar.

Perhaps it had been the meeting with his father, or the fact that while Liam was gone Michael was also overseeing the winery—well, at least supervising the executive staff, who normally reported to Liam—but he'd wanted a break. Today was one of those days where if he put out one fire, another would ignite.

He lifted his drink, and for the first time since he'd climbed out of bed, allowed himself to relax. He'd even silenced his phone notifications. He wanted good food, but he hadn't wanted to eat at Miller's Grill by himself and wanted more than the self-serve wine bar's charcuterie board offerings. As the evening was mild and pleasant, he'd walked north from his apartment to the bar district, and then, as if drawn by an invisible pull, he'd entered Kaiser's. Unlike Halloween, when the place had been packed, tonight it was half-full, with diners enjoying drinks and dinner.

"What can I get you?" The same bartender as before approached. She wore a slightly quizzical look, one that made Michael wonder if she recognized him from Halloween or if she knew he was Michael Clayton, cousin to Jack, the owner of the building. It wasn't as if the Clayton family hadn't been pictured in the Beaumont community newspaper on multiple occasions, like when they'd donated the land to save the bats. Clayton Holdings also bought a full back-page ad in the town's free weekly publication.

Instead of ordering bourbon, beer or wine, Michael opted for one of the locally brewed hard ciders on draft. The bartender slid the tall glass filled with golden-red liquid toward him. "Would you like a menu?"

"Please." Michael sipped the delicious cider while

he perused the dinner options. When the bartender returned he ordered a chopped salad containing romaine lettuce, bacon, tomatoes, avocados, smoked brisket and blue-cheese crumbles. Served with a creamy mustard-based dressing, his first forkful was delicious.

"How is everything?" the bartender asked after he'd eaten several bites.

Michael washed the bite with a sip of cider. "Good. Exactly what I wanted."

"Glad to hear it. Are you meeting anyone?" she asked.

Michael glanced around. While a few others sat at the bar, there were plenty of empty stools. "Not that I know of. Should I be?"

"Haven't seen you in here since Halloween," she said. "When you were with my friend."

"Ah." She had recognized him. That night Ione had told him that she knew the owner. *Cordelia*. The bartender's name came back. Ione had told him a little about her and her upcoming nuptials. Had Ione told Cordelia what had happened between them? "I've been busy," he told her.

"Most of us are. But I'm not one for coincidences," Cordelia said. Her straight, dark blond hair was pulled back in a long ponytail, and her lips had puckered. Michael got the impression he'd done something wrong, not that he knew what it was.

"I don't understand." He ate another bite and sipped more cider, but Cordelia didn't say anything. "Do you want me to ask how Ione is?" Michael queried, to fill the silence.

"Oh, so you remember her name."

"Why wouldn't I?" Michael asked, his brow creasing. He hadn't expected this vibe when he'd come in here. Maybe he should box up the salad and leave, as it seemed clear Cordelia knew about his and Ione's hookup. "I asked for her contact information but she chose not to give it to me."

Cordelia folded her arms, her diamond engagement ring reflecting the light as she studied him. "It's the truth," Michael defended. "I respected her wishes. Did I do something wrong?"

"Well, luckily for you, she didn't know who you were or your reputation, and I chose not to tell her once I learned of it. Your cousin raising our rent makes you problematic enough."

"Wait, what?"

"Our rent went up. As for the rest," Cordelia said with a head tilt toward the door, "you can ask her yourself, because there she is now."

Like a thirsty man being offered a glass of water, Michael watched Ione enter the bar. She didn't pause as she saw him, and Michael realized her friend had warned her of his presence. He was grateful for that small favor. Only one of them needed to be as shocked as he currently felt.

"Hi, Michael," she said. He noted her smile seemed hesitant and shy. She wasn't as unaffected as she was pretending to be. "How are you?"

"Good. Fine. Great. You look great." He babbled the truth like a starstruck fool. In a concession to the warmer weather, she wore a short-sleeve sweater that accented breasts he'd palmed with abandon. Her jeans fit low on her hips, and a hint of stomach showed when she sat one stool away, leaving a full person's worth of space between them. "You've been well? How was West Virginia?" He'd been there several times over the past six months visiting various Clayton Hotels. Not that he'd stayed long, but enough to think of her.

She moved her fingers as if to touch her curly dark blond hair before checking the motion and dropping the hand into her lap. "West Virginia was fine. I did some hiking. Finished the project. I saw you donated the land."

"It was a brilliant idea." Michael watched Cordelia slide a glass of white wine toward Ione. "Thank you for making the suggestion."

She lifted her glass. "You're welcome. Glad I could help. The bats deserve their habitat."

"My siblings and I agreed with you, Liam especially."

Unable to tear his gaze away, he watched her lips form words. "Ah, yes, Liam. He's quite the environmentalist."

"He is."

When she lifted her wine in avoidance of saying anything else, Michael took another bite of salad, which kept him from watching her. He needed his wits about him. He'd encountered plenty of former lovers after the fact. Since they came from his social circle, everyone knew the score. They knew how to navigate the social niceties of whatever situation they found themselves in. But he'd broken the rules with Ione.

He'd met her in a bar—this very bar—and taken her home. The only thing he'd known about her was that he wanted her enough to break his newly made vow to turn over a new leaf. The night had been everything he'd wanted and more. Seeing her now brought back the softness of her sighs, the deepness of her moans, the way she'd clung to him and the way her blue eyes had widened as he'd filled her.

The overwhelming need to talk to her, to process what had happened between them, was a sensation Michael had never experienced. Before he'd met Ione, one night had meant one night. In her case, that night had gotten under his skin. He'd been unable to forget her. Maybe it was because he'd followed her advice to donate the land. He took another bite, highly aware that Ione had slid off the stool. She leaned forward over the bar top so that she and Cordelia could bend their heads together and hold a whispered conversation.

Michael lifted his glass and drained the last of his cider in one long gulp. Wasn't like he was driving. Although, after being stored for the winter, the Corvette was once again parked behind the art gallery next to the fully electric Cadillac SUV he'd purchased. He hadn't yet found a house, but he was okay with that. Eva had showed him several, but none had felt right. He pushed his plate forward. He'd eaten most of the salad and didn't want to box up the rest. He rose and dropped enough cash onto the bar to cover his bill. Time to cede the floor and do something he'd never done before. Flee.

As Michael moved past her with a "it was good to see you," Ione remained rooted, since she was so stunned by the fact he was leaving. By the time she'd jerked around from speaking with Cordelia so that she could face him directly, Michael had already reached the door. By the time she made to call him back, he was outside. The door closed with a thud.

"Wipe that horrified expression off your face," Cordelia ordered as she removed Michael's plates from the bar top. "You did nothing wrong, and don't you dare think of chasing after him."

"That did not go as I'd planned." Settling back onto her stool, Ione swallowed another sip of chardonnay. "What must he think of me?"

"Who says he's been thinking of you at all? You sent me the pictures. He's with someone else. He's a playboy, Ione. Always has been. Your night meant nothing to him. If I'd realized you were going to proposition him and go home with him, I would have told you who he was that night before you left the bar. As it was, I kept my mouth closed since you didn't seem too affected. But here you are, all googly eyed, which is why I told you before you arrived today."

"You did tell me to move on from Henry."

"But not with a Clayton. They aren't like us. They're not even in our orbit."

Ione sighed. "It was just such a dream night. I'll get over it eventually."

"Of course, because life's a series of small and big moments, with many harder than others, and this one is not as big in reality as it is in your mind. Can you pretend it never happened?"

"Didn't I already do that? Don't I have to do that? I'm going to be working for them so I have to be professional. I'd ask to be reassigned but there's literally no one else. And my mom needs me. We'll be fine."

Even if after seeing her, he'd run away as fast as his strong, muscular legs could carry him. Legs that had cradled her as he'd driven her to heights unexpected? Ione cringed. So much for reunions. While she'd expected him to ignore what had occurred between them, his leaving felt like stinging rejection.

Worse, even though Cordelia had warned her of his presence via cryptic text, Ione hadn't been ready for how her body had reacted when she'd seen him. He'd looked wonderful. Hair that had been silky under her touch had recently been cut. Gray eyes she'd stared into remained deep, expressive and mysterious. When the full lips that had kissed her senseless had wrapped around a fork, her body had given a tiny shiver. He even made chewing an art form.

"Snap out of it," Cordelia said, her fingers making the motion for added emphasis. "He's just a man. He's not worth a second thought. You have a job to do."

"I know." But saying the words was like stopping El Niño. Ione slid her empty glass forward. Cordelia uncorked the bottle, a Clayton Holdings white blend from one of the company wineries located in Washington State. "I've seen him, so it'll be easier next time. I doubt he'll attend the meetings. He's a VP." She shook her head. "A VP. What was I thinking? Why didn't you tell me?"

"Because you're an adult and I thought you knew better. Because after the fact it wouldn't have helped much and instead given you something else to obsess over." Cordelia sighed and changed subjects. "How's your mom?"

"I'm worried, but Arwen says she's as stubborn as ever, which is good, as it means she's fighting. I don't want her to give up. This time her ovarian cancer is pretty aggressive, and it's taking a toll both mentally and physically. Not that she'll tell me or my sister that, but I'm her health-care power of attorney. I read the reports. I should have come back to Beaumont more often, not just for a quick visit at Christmas."

Cordelia gave Ione's had a squeeze. "Oh, honey. What can I do?"

"Nothing. She's on the list for an experimental treatment. Since it's not covered by insurance, when she gets it it's going to cost a lot of money. Luckily, I've saved up. My job pays well, especially with the quarterly bonuses for completed projects."

Ione sipped more wine. "I can work remotely once I've been with the firm a year, so I'll move back once my lease is up. It's not like I'm ever there." Currently she had a tiny apartment in Atlanta, since the company headquarters was located there and the airport was a hub for the carrier she flew the most.

"If you need a fundraiser, you tell me," Cordelia insisted. "You shouldn't have to spend your own money. She probably hates that."

"I think she'd hate more the fact the town knows her issues and believes her to be a charity case. I've got it covered." A bit of a stretch, but Ione would get the finances handled. "Tell me about your issues. What's going on? I know when something's troubling you. I might not be able to read people well, but I can read you."

Cordelia poured two glasses of red wine before passing them to a server. "We have two issues. One, we're not meeting the food minimums the city set for Kaiser's. If we can't do that, we're going to have to shut down. Two, the rent increased in January. We've been hanging on, but barely. You know this place has been in my family for generations, but I'm wondering if I should let it go.

I went to college. Did I really get an MBA just to sling drinks? Or have my fiancé cook?"

Before Cordelia went to wipe the bar top, it was Ione's turn to provide the reassuring hand squeeze. "What can I do?"

Cordelia managed a small smile. "Give me the best wedding shower ever. Three weeks until I marry the man of my dreams. That's all that matters. The rest will work itself out. I have to believe that."

The phone at the end of the bar began shrilling, and the noise was joined by the sound of sirens coming from the fire station up the road. Because of the rural nature of Beaumont County, a group of trained volunteers supplemented the fire department's full-time staff.

Cordelia answered the landline and Ione watched her face pale. "What is it?" Ione demanded once Cordelia returned the receiver to its cradle. Something was wrong and Ione was around the bar as fast as her legs could go.

Her friend began to tremble. "It's the Annex. It's on fire."

"What? No!" But Ione's phone pinged with a text message from her sister saying the same thing. It was amazing how fast news traveled through the Beaumont grapevine on a normal day, but disastrous news like this traveled especially fast. The Annex was a lovely stone barn on the Meyersburg Farm that played host to dozens of weddings a year. Cordelia's was supposed to be held there in three weeks' time.

The key word being *was*. As Ione watched the video her sister sent of the historic building filled with flames, Cordelia's phone beeped with the same video. "Don't watch that," Ione commanded, plucking the phone from Cordelia's hand. "Whatever you do, don't watch that."

"It's ruined. There's no way it will be fixed."

"No, it will be fine." Ione gathered Cordelia in her arms as her friend began to cry. "You know Will would marry you in a field or in the courthouse because he loves you and that's what matters. And, yes, I know that's not the point."

Will came out from the kitchen. He wiped his hands on his apron and Ione stepped back so he could gather Cordelia in his arms. "I already called my brothers," he told Ione. "As soon as they get here, I'm going to take her home."

Ione had never been good at handling emotions. She was a problem solver. Her skill set lay in finding solutions to the unsolvable. She might not understand social subtleties, but she was the one who was able to get things done when others couldn't. She found answers when there were none. Like how to save bats. Or eagles. Or weddings.

"I'm going to fix it," she told Cordelia. "I promise you, I'm going to fix it."

Ione knew just the person to ask.

Chapter Four

When Michael opened the door to his apartment later that evening, he thought he knew who might be standing there. Instead, he found himself pleasantly surprised. "Hey." He stepped back to let Ione pass, which gave him both a maddening view of her backside and a whiff of that outdoorsy, floral sent so unique to her. Even after six months, her presence called to him in the way no other woman had. "What are you doing here?" he asked as they climbed the stairs. From the way she'd ignored him at Kaiser's he certainly hadn't expected to see her again. She whirled around once in his living room. Her trembling lips revealed she was upset about something.

"Have I done something wrong? Have I hurt you?" He hoped not. "You know you can tell me whatever it is."

"I need your help," she said without preamble, which made Michael's gut clench. "The Annex is on fire."

Okay, that was not the news he was expecting. "You mean the place on Meyersburg Farm?"

"Yes. It's a total loss. How do you not know already? Didn't you hear the sirens?"

"I saw a truck go by." He tried to figure out how this was connected to him. Normally when a woman appeared unannounced on his doorstep, she was there to accuse him of something or plead for another chance. Remembering he'd silenced his phone, he rummaged in his pocket. Finding it, he saw he had a half-dozen texts, most from hotel managers. The Annex was a premier wedding venue. Not on the glamourous level of the Chateau, but in a quaint, rustic way. "I can't believe it caught on fire."

"Well, it did."

Michael understood the implications. If the building was a total loss, as Ione had said, any weddings the Annex had scheduled would need to be relocated. Since the Annex didn't have its own lodgings, wedding parties and their guests often stayed at the Beaumont Grand. Cancellations would negatively impact room occupancy. The Grand and the Chateau were also booked solid with their own onsite weddings. Most of the messages were from Clayton Hotels wedding coordinators and several managers. Already his staff had fielded phone calls from anxious brides needing a new venue. What were they to do?

Yet another fire—this one literal—he had to deal with.

"Losing a wedding venue is not good. But it'll be okay." Ione planted her hands on her hips and leaned forward. Michael knew he'd said the wrong thing, and unsure why, worked to reassure her. "The Annex's insurance company will refund deposits and work with brides to find alternative venues. It's not ideal, but this happened once in Portland and that's what they did."

Ione began to pace, her gestures still erratic. "One of those weddings you're so nonchalant about is Cordelia's. *In three weeks.*"

Crap. Michael winced. Now, he understood why Ione was so agitated. "I'm sorry."

Before he could say more, she continued. "I need to fix this. You have to help me. I can't let Cordelia suffer. I'm her maid of honor."

Ione's distress twisted a knife inside him. "I can tell my managers to prioritize Cordelia's wedding over other brides, but I know our hotels are fully booked. My wedding coordinators are already texting me with dozens of questions. I'll meet with them, as well as the wedding coordinators for the wineries, to see how many ceremonies and receptions we can handle—"

Ione cut him off. "I'm the maid of honor. I promised her I'd fix this. I *have* to fix it." She stopped and stared at him as if seeing him for the first time. "I need your help. You owe me."

How many times had he heard those last three words, even from his own father? Michael's hackles rose. "I'm not letting you blackmail me because we had sex."

Ione's face morphed into an expression of disgust. "What? No. I can't believe you'd even suggest that. The fact we were intimate is that last thing I want people to know. Do you think I like being yet another conquest of the notorious Portland Playboy? It's not a badge of honor. Had I known… That doesn't matter now. What's done is done."

Michael winced as the moniker the press had given him exited Ione's mouth. Never had he hated his past more, especially because now she regretted the best night of his life.

"You owe me for my help for with your bats. I solved

your problem. Turnabout's only fair. I helped you. You help me. Solve mine."

"Oh. The bats." The conversation had taken a strange turn. Miffed she'd dismissed and cheapened a night he couldn't forget by calling him a playboy, which he hadn't been since meeting her, he folded his arms across his chest. He wouldn't let her see how her words had wounded him. "Do fill me in as to why you making an offhand suggestion in a bar gives you the right to ask things of me."

Committed to her quest, she didn't miss a beat. "Because that offhand suggestion fixed your problem. You got my expertise for free. It was clearly worthwhile, as you hired Good-4 Environmental to handle the land donation and rehired them to fix your eagle problem and oversee the construction of all the pollinator habitats."

Michael's shock was audible and he snapped out, "How could you possibly know that?"

Besides his father and several executives, no one else knew that his firm had inked the new contract a few days ago. Eva hadn't yet put the news out to the media, as Michael had wanted to wait until after they'd met with the consultant and had a firm plan for the eagles in place. Michael found it was his turn to pace. "How do you have that type of insider information?"

"Because I'm your consultant." When he stopped short, Ione shoved her hand forward. "Dr. Hermione Scott, at your service."

Okay, he hadn't seen that twist coming, and without thinking, Michael automatically took her hand. Warmth fused their fingers together as he peered into her blue eyes, outlined with a thin line of darker blue. "You said your name was Ione."

She didn't avert her gaze, and her chin rose. "It's short for Hermione. After the character in *Harry Potter*. My mom named her children after characters in literature. My sister is Arwen from *Lord of the Rings*. And I still need you to help Cordelia."

"From *Buffy the Vampire Slayer*."

An eyebrow arched and her head tilted slightly. "Yes."

The fact he knew that added one point in his favor, at least. Another was that she hadn't pulled away, meaning her hand remained in his. Her palm perfect against his skin, a tingling sensation traveled through his arm. Desire settled in his groin and he shifted his weight. Whatever this chemistry was between them, it hadn't lessened since last October. "Nice to meet you officially, Hermione who goes by Ione. I think I like thinking of you as a Greek nymph better than a bookish wizard."

Her long lashes fluttered furiously as she blinked. "I solved your bat problem. Granted, I didn't know who you were, but I was working for Good-4 Environmental when I did. That puts me in an ethical dilemma, especially as we had sex. An even worse dilemma, as it seems you have a lot of indiscriminate sex. I never would have slept with you had I known."

"So you keep saying. You should be aware that the media tends to exaggerate my nocturnal activities." She stared at him like he was lying, and it irritated him. "I'm tired of the stigma."

"Exaggerated or not, the fact remains that we *did* have sex. A one-night stand. That matters to me."

"It matters to me, too, but there's nothing wrong with

a one-night stand between consenting adults, which we were."

"I never said there was. It's the aftermath that's the problem."

He was having difficulty following her logic, which probably meant she thought he was a jerk. "I'm not sure how our physical activities could be considered a conflict of interest. Clayton Holdings wasn't working with your firm at that time. We didn't exchange contact information. As for moving forward, no one will think twice about seeing us together, since no one knows of our involvement."

"Cordelia knows. She's my best friend."

"Which I understand." Women talked to their friends, which was how he'd been set up to kiss his former girlfriend's bestie. "But I'm assuming she's discreet."

"Of course, she is. Which is why I want your help." Ione frowned at him and he didn't like it. He wanted the old Ione back, the one whose soft sighs and honest responses to his touch had given him the best night of his life.

As if realizing they hadn't let go of each other, she removed her hand from his, causing the tingles to cease. "Everyone knows that the Clayton family runs everything in Beaumont. If anyone can perform a miracle, it's you. I'm a fixer. I need to fix this."

"Do you even believe in miracles?" Michael asked, unable to help himself. It was better than thinking that Ione had turned into yet another person who needed something from him because of his last name.

She stepped away. "No, or my mother would be cancer-free. Instead she's a shell of herself."

"I'm sorry. I genuinely am." He was a heel for not giving her the benefit of the doubt.

"Thank you." Her chest heaved as she regained control over her runaway emotions. "As for miracles, there are some things science can't explain. If those are miracles, I need one. I'll repay any help you can give. I'll help you with your eagle problem, by doing some overtime. I could even add some upgrades to your pollinator project, since I'm taking that over. I'm making a fair offer for your time and assistance. Do we have a deal?"

"We don't need a deal. I said I'd help." What he wanted right now was to drop the entire subject. He didn't like seeing her stressed.

"Thank you. That's all I want."

What he wanted, he couldn't have. He wanted to pull her back into his arms and kiss her senseless. He wanted to carry her off to his bed and see if their first night had been a fluke. If it had, perhaps he could forget it. Purge it from living rent-free in his head.

But absconding like a caveman with Ione was off-limits, would be a true conflict of interest, and it would make him the absolute worst kind of man, the one whom he was wanting to leave firmly in the past.

"I can't make you any promises, but I'll see what I can do. I'll be meeting with my wedding staff, since the managers are already asking how we're going to handle things. And the buck stops with me. I'll make Cordelia's wedding a priority, not because I owe you, or because you helped me, but because that night mattered to me. *You* matter to me."

Edmund and Liam had always maintained that being a Clayton meant being able to make things happen. Maybe it was Michael's turn to do something for a woman besides whisking her off for a long weekend on the private jet. Pre-Ione, of course. "I can assure you I'll look into Cordelia's situation personally. But you'll need to give me the details, which means I need your contact information."

Visibly relieved, Ione softened and lost some of her forcefulness. "Thank you. I'm sorry for the way I came across, as if I was attacking you. I'm just so upset for her."

"I understand. I'm glad you came to me." Even if it hurt that she hadn't acknowledged that he'd told her she mattered to him. But he also knew that's how her brain worked. She was in an analytical, crisis-solving mode for the people she loved. He admired how she put them first and knew one night didn't move him into a friendship category. But he hoped maybe he'd get there. He wanted that, at least.

"I'm grateful that you're going to try," Ione said softly. "I know that's all I can ask. It's important that I help her because she's taken a lot of hits lately. Your cousin raised the rent on all the Main Street properties last January. Kaiser's isn't selling enough food, so Cordelia might lose the business if she can't meet the city's food threshold. You got a lot of good publicity from the bats, you could get a lot more from this. Cordelia is a beloved town icon. That bar has been in her family for four generations."

Jack had raised the rents? Michael's cousin had been about helping merchants stay in business. When had that changed? Michael added talking to his cousin to his ever-growing mental list of things to do. A loss of any business could hurt Clayton Holdings's vision for the region, especially as visiting the historic downtown was a huge tourist draw, essential for the entire area. "It's true we got a lot of good PR out of donating the land. You did me a solid with your suggestion. I'll try my best to repay the favor."

"Those bats needed saving."

That was Ione, always putting nature first. Another point in her ever-growing plus column. "The bats did," he agreed, resisting the urge to tuck one of those wild curls behind her ear. "It was the right thing to do. Can I ask you a question? How are you? I hoped I might run into you again if you came back to Beaumont." He'd thought he'd seen her at Christmas, but when he'd taken a closer look, she'd been gone. Must have been a wistful figment of his imagination.

Her face turned toward his, but before he could ask her thoughts about the night they'd spent together, his doorbell buzzed.

Like a frightened rabbit, she readied to bolt. "Oh, my. I interrupted. You have company. Your date. I saw your picture online. She's pretty. I should go. I'll see you tomorrow."

"Ione, can we please…" She was far more important than whoever was outside.

But she was already on the wooden stairs, and he followed hard on her heels. He wasn't fast enough to stop her from leaving, and he heard rather than saw her as she said, "Oh, hello" to the woman stepping inside. Once on the landing, he stuck his head out and watched as Ione fled around the corner. Great. Just great. Could this day get any worse?

Of course, it could. With Amy's arrival, he couldn't chase after Ione.

"Who was that?" Amy asked. She eased by him, leaving a waft of expensive perfume in her wake that almost made Michael sneeze. "You did remember I was coming by, didn't you? And that we were going out?"

He had, and he'd expected her when he'd opened the door to Ione. He stared at Amy as if seeing her for the first time, even though they'd had five dates, all of which had ended with chaste kisses on the cheek and nothing more. Amy was beautiful, her brown hair perfectly styled and her makeup subtle.

Ione's curls had been wild, her face bare and naturally beautiful. Showing up as she had showed guts. Her asking for his help was rooted in a desire to help her friend. She'd been thinking of Cordelia and trying to make things right. As Amy pushed a strand of hair back, Michael thought of how Ione's dark blond waves had cascaded to her shoulders like a wild sea nymph, triggering the memory of how those strands had appeared spread out against his pillows. He wanted to see them there again. He could never feel that way about the woman in front of him, despite her being a good person. He couldn't do to her what he'd done with Rachel back in Portland—continue something when his heart would never be in it. That wasn't fair to her. He wouldn't lead her on.

Once in the living room, Amy turned, her face angled for a kiss that Michael had no desire to bestow, so he didn't. Instead, he gave her the words no woman wanted to hear, but words he needed to say now that Ione had walked back into his life.

"Amy, we need to talk."

* * *

After she left Michael's apartment, Ione ordered a car. Her suite at the Beaumont Grand had a separate living room and oversize bedroom, but because she'd seen Michael, the walls felt far too confining. She polished her presentation one more time before settling on the couch. She flipped through the TV channels, pausing once when she recognized one of the recent *Ghostbusters* movies. Even watching fake supernatural evil get blasted and trapped into containment units didn't divert her from her melancholy. Michael had said she'd mattered. The words had shocked her so much she hadn't been able to respond, and by the time the giddiness began to break through the intensity of their conversation, his girlfriend had shown up. Ione rested her feet on the ottoman. She needed to remember she was here to work, not flirt or carry on with Michael. She also had to help her mom. Wondering how she was, Ione sent her and Arwen texts. Both went unread. She'd make a point to visit tomorrow, after her meetings. She doubted Michael would be in attendance. Surely, he had better things to do. Like talk to his girlfriend. Ione pushed aside the bitterness. She'd seen their pictures on the internet. She had no reason to be jealous. She and Michael didn't have anything but one night ages ago. But, of course, he'd chosen one of those women with bow lips, perfectly arched eyebrows, high chiseled cheekbones, wide eyes, balanced facial symmetry and the innate sense of style Ione lacked.

While Ione knew she could outclimb, outski and outpaddle the brunette, she couldn't outshine her. She'd never been a traditional beauty. Her dark blond hair was too unruly, her body too tall and sporty. She'd been the volleyball player and the science geek, not the cheerleader. She resisted the urge to burden Cordelia with these latest events. Instead, she sent a message telling her that she was at the hotel and to call if she needed anything. While Ione could see that Cordelia had read the text, no response was forthcoming. After suffering the blow of your wedding venue burning down, Ione didn't expect a return text for a while.

Ione blew out an exasperated puff of air. Not enough to carry her frustration away, but the force did send one of her curls bouncing. She turned off the TV and rose. The hotel had opened its outdoor pool, so one option was to swim and work out her feelings that way. Maybe she should run along the paved paths that led around the property. Or she could go downstairs and have a drink and dinner, something she'd planned to do at Kaiser's.

At least the bridal shower was already set. Ione had chosen to hold the event at Elephant Rock, one of Clayton Holding's area wineries. Unlike the more upscale Jamestown, Elephant Rock was a casual place preferred by cyclists riding along the Katy Trail. One of Will and Cordelia's first dates had been a twenty-mile bike ride that had ended at Elephant Rock. Ione had secured the winery's pavilion months ago, and using ideas researched on Pinterest, she had created and sent invitations. She'd ordered supplies and a cake, and she'd delegated decorations and games to Cordelia's other bridesmaids. Nothing would go wrong this upcoming Sunday—Ione would see to it.

Right now, though, she needed to get out of the room before her thoughts turned once again to Michael. She grabbed her phone, checked that her wallet was magnified to the back and that she had her room key. She reached the door and pulled it open. "Oh!"

Michael stood there wearing the same clothes as earlier, dress slacks and a dark blue polo that emphasized how handsome he was. "What are you doing here?"

He hovered a few feet away from the doorway. "I came to talk to you. Sorry. I didn't mean to scare you. I should have texted first. Are you leaving?"

"I was going downstairs to the bar to have dinner."

He dragged a hand through his hair. "Mind if I join you?"

"Didn't you just eat?" Ione poked her head around him and glanced both ways down the empty hallway. "Where's your girlfriend?"

He made to drag his hand through his hair again but stopped himself. "She's not my girlfriend. Never was. Never even kissed her."

"Really? That's hard to believe."

Michael's shoulders drooped with resignation. "With my reputation, yeah, I deserve that. The truth is that we went on a few dates. I told her today there won't be any more. Will you let me explain?"

"You're allowed to have a life." She still didn't understand why he was here, and part of her toyed with the thrilling idea that he'd chased after her so he could explain. But what did that mean? "I don't think an explanation is necessary. It might even muddle things more."

"My goal is to clear things up. There's been no one since you, Ione. No one. No one in my bed but me."

Ione shut a mouth that had dropped open. She fought to control the excited shiver that powered through her.

No one? How was that possible? Especially with his vitality and virility? According to the press, women threw themselves at him. How could he have been celibate as long as she had? Because if true, the revelation had serious implications. Already, her body responded to his. She longed to trace his jaw. Smooth his brow. She opened the door wider. "Come in."

Michael shifted from side to side. "Only if we can talk. I feel like we got off on the wrong foot earlier. We can go downstairs if you'd like."

She thought fast. "We don't want to look like we're on a date, especially since you were seen with someone else not that long ago."

His mouth twisted. "And you're worried about that?"

"Yes. We can call this a business meeting."

"Ione, you don't have anything to fear."

"I know. It's not about that." She wished she hadn't sounded so ridiculous. But being near him made her nervous. She wasn't afraid of what he might do, but rather her own lack of self-control. She'd gone to his apartment and badgered him, something out of character for her, despite her admittedly unpolished social skills. Even propositioning him Halloween weekend had been an aberration, a step outside her normal comfort zone. The adage Throw Caution to the Wind suddenly made sense.

Ione gestured Michael inside and closed the door. He strode into the living room, filling the area with his presence. He stepped farther away as if to give her needed space. "I see you've set up your laptop. We assigned you a suite so that you could have a secondary place to work. While you'll have an office at Clayton Holdings, our employees often work from home. I thought it might be good to be closer to the eagles' nest and be able to experience what we do here at our properties. All things that were decided before I knew you were our consultant."

"That makes sense. Thank you. It's nice to have a living space and not worry about anything."

"And I worry about everything." Michael heaved a tired sigh. "Sorry, it's been a long day with one crisis after another. The fire added one more layer."

Guilt shot through her like an arrow. "Now, I feel bad. I gave you something else to deal with by asking you to help me. And I came across as rude."

"You wanted to help your friend. If I were in your shoes, I'd have done the same. It's fine. No harm done."

"Still, I shouldn't have badgered you. I acted without thinking." Like she had when she'd asked him to take her to bed. "I was impulsive." Normally a rarity for a woman as tightly wound as she was.

"We all do that, so don't beat yourself up. Seriously."

She couldn't let it go. "Still. It was wrong and I apologize."

"Think no more of it. Just let me clear the air. While I might have acted like a playboy at times when I was younger, it's also true that my reputation is highly overblown."

Part of her wanted to believe that, but Henry said all sorts of sweet things that had turned out to be massive nothings, including that he loved her. He'd made false promises, saying that they might marry one day. He'd blamed the relationship's failure on her. Worse, people had believed him. That had been one reason she'd moved into private consulting postbreakup. He'd had seniority, and while his public outburst could have brought discipline, the process would have been cumbersome. Far easier to turn tail and leave.

"I'm sorry I called you a playboy. I say things without thinking sometimes. That was uncalled for."

"Thank you, although you don't need to apologize." His lips twisted. "And it sounds like there's a *but* coming."

He already knew her so well. "There is. In my line of work, sometimes companies hire Good-4 Environmental for the wrong reasons. They want us cover up their misdeeds, or give them plausible deniability. They want to cut corners. They figure paying some hefty fine later will cost less than doing the right thing from the start. If that happens, we, as consultants, can be blamed for the fallout. It happened to my predecessor. I can't afford to be caught in any bad press. Which you seem to attract."

"True."

She nibbled her lip before catching herself. "I can tell Clayton Holdings is different, especially since your brother is a proven environmentalist. But I had a company try to burn me once. Before that, I had a colleague succeed in it, which is why I'm now in the private sector. That makes me cautious. It's why I research my clients. I don't like surprises, especially ones that could sully my reputation and by association that of Good-4 Environmental."

"Thank you for understanding that's not Clayton Holdings," Michael said. "Maybe decades ago when my dad and uncle were starting out things were different, that was long before we understood man's impact on the environment. Edmund and Liam have pushed us even more in the right direction."

"Which I admire. Clayton Holdings has become one of the leaders in sustainability in the hospitality industry. You're known for doing the right thing from the start. But your personal reputation, whether true or not, means I must stay professional. If people see me working with you after hours, what would they think?"

"Why does it matter? I know what I think. I think you were never simply one night to me. I need you to realize that. Okay?"

Chapter Five

After the words left his lips, Michael wished he could call them back. But he couldn't. He'd shocked her. She touched her throat. "I know you're serious. But why?"

He had a million reasons but settled on the most basic. "Why? Because I still want you. Because you, Ione, drive me a little bit crazy in a way I want to explore."

"I see." He could tell she didn't. But he could also tell she felt the full impact of his words. As she held his gaze, something inside him shifted. If there was a moment he could fall in love with Ione, this might be it. Or at least it was the moment he gave her the power to break his heart or lead him like a lamb to slaughter.

He couldn't get her out of his head, nor did he want to. Unlike others, she wanted nothing from him. She was pure, unvarnished perfection. Too bad in her eyes he was the clichéd playboy who had managed to ruin things before they could even start. He couldn't abide that. "You were never one more notch on my bedpost. Emphasis on the *never*. And it's certainly not my intention to sully your reputation. Either professionally or personally."

Her blue eyes widened. Resisting the urge to trace a lower lip that had dropped open, Michael pointed to the door. "Do you want me to leave? Meet you some-where else?"

"We're fine sitting in here so long as your staff is discreet."

"It's the Beaumont Grand."

He realized he'd said the wrong thing when her wor-ried expression stayed put. "I don't know what that means."

He loved how blunt she was. She was a fresh breeze in his jaded world. "It means no one will say a thing. Our hotels are known for discretion and privacy, which is one reason so many celebrities stay with us. Our hotels are simply the best in the world. And now I sound like a cliché, boasting like that." He paused. "You don't think I'm making fun of you, do you? That's not my intention."

"No." A quick headshake helped convince him. "I learned how to read the signals when people are doing that." She straightened. "I can see what you're thinking. Don't pity me. I hate people's pity. It's annoying when people find me lacking because I don't play games or catch subtleties." She gestured. "Your world is not my world. I don't understand the dynamics or what to ex-pect."

"I'll guide you through it." He would.

"When you do, I need you to be straight with me at all times, even if you think it'll hurt me."

"I can do that. And my world is frankly often absurd. There are days I don't like the fakery myself." Michael swiped open his cell phone and held it out. "I know you worry about propriety, so let's eat in. Finish our con-versation. Here's the room-service menu. What do you want for dinner?"

Ione didn't take the phone. "I have an expense account."

"Ione." Michael thrust the device forward. "Clayton Hotels is paying for the consultant's room and meals. Until a few days before we met last October, I was living in one of the penthouses. I constantly dialed room service because I'm a terrible cook who burns microwavable meals. Please look at the menu and choose something. If I order it directly, it'll arrive faster. That way, I'll leave faster. I'm not trying to be rude. Just direct, like you asked."

"What you said was perfect." Her shoulders relaxed and she gave him a small smile that acted like a slingshot, shooting hope at him, even though he knew that was a silly assumption. But he wanted her to like him.

"I'm glad I did it right."

"The more direct you are, the better," she said. "I like statistics. Facts. Paper trails. It's something that makes me good at my job. Cordelia once described me as being more Mr. Spock than Captain Kirk. I'm logical."

"I happen to like Mr. Spock."

Their fingers touched as she took his phone, and he resisted the urge to clasp her hand in his. He wanted to pull her to him and press her against a body longing for more. She glanced over the menu and handed back his phone. "I'd like the French dip with fries and a small side salad."

"Any dessert?" When she hesitated, he said, "I'll order a small cookie tray. If nothing else, I could use something sweet after the day I've had. My father amped up the pressure. He's always micromanaging. It's his favorite pastime. You'll see that tomorrow."

"Will I be meeting with him?"

"You very well might be. But don't worry. I'll run interference."

"You'll be there?" She worried her lower lip with her teeth again.

"Yes, and you'll be great. You've got this. I trust you."

With that, Michael walked toward the door, punched in a number, put the phone to his ear and talked low. While he ordered, he noted Ione sat in a wingback chair. When he returned, he grabbed waters from the mini-fridge and moved to the sofa.

"Hey." He slid a bottle across the coffee table toward her. "Shall we try this reunion thing again? Because I would like to be friends."

"Is that possible? I'm not friends with my exes." Ione gripped her knees, the khaki pants she wore wrinkling under her fingers. "But friends sounds nice."

"Come to think of it, I don't think I'm friends with any of mine, either. So maybe this can be a new path for both of us. You can trust me. I'm not going to bite." He ignored the images of the way he'd nipped his way down her neck.

That earned him more of a smile. "I know that. You were the consummate gentleman." Her face flamed that shade of pink he'd seen all over her body. "And lover. I want to tell you that before we move to the just-friends stuff. You constantly asked my permission before you did something. I appreciated that. It was nice."

Nice. He loved her simple word choice. "If we're being honest, it was spectacular."

"And sexy," she countered.

That word got his attention, and he managed not to groan. "You don't know what you do to me, do you?"

"No." She was honest to a fault, which he adored.

"You turn me on in a way no one else does. But I'm shoving all that back in the proverbial box so we can at least be friends."

"Okay. What happens next? Because I'm nervous about the presentation tomorrow if your father's going to be there."

"Give him straight answers and you'll be fine. That's all he wants. And we simply take things one step at a time. We don't have to tell people about our past, but I don't want to be some dirty secret, either." He added the last part casually. Ione reminded him of a deer he'd spooked once when driving along Winery Road late at night. She could bolt at any moment, when what he really wanted was to get to know her.

She chewed her lower lip and swiped it with her forefinger, as if trying to desensitize the nerves. "I'll try. I never thought I'd be in this situation. In the past, how have you handle your one-night stands? Maybe that can be a blueprint for us."

Michael choked on the water he'd been drinking. "Uh... Um..."

Ione pressed forward. "Surely you've seen the women you've slept with socially afterward. Like the one today."

"I told you I didn't sleep with her. I haven't slept with anyone since you. I wasn't lying about that. I won't lie to you. That's a promise I'll make you right now."

She tilted her head and he could sense she was considering his words. "I appreciate that. When I got to

Beaumont, I figured we'd pretend what happened never happened, but today showed me we can't."

Michael realized she was out of her wheelhouse. "Ignoring each other only works when people don't want to hook up again. I can't say that."

"You want to have sex with me…again?" Her blue eyes widened. "Seriously? Why?"

"Because I like you." Her self-doubt surprised and bothered him. "And because you're awesome. Because the sex we had was unlike anything else." He fiddled with the label wrapped around the water bottle, his finger sliding under the plastic and creating a crunching sound. "Because I'm wondering if it was a fluke. Or more importantly, if it could be the start of something even better."

She studied a fingernail instead of looking at him. "I'm not your type."

"I get to be the judge of that. Stop trying to make yourself less in my eyes. I can see you all on my own, and I like what I see. Do you like what you see?"

Her head came up. "Yes. I can agree the sex was better than with my previous two lovers, so I understand why I might want to have sex with you again. You're far more experienced and knew what to do."

Two lovers. His own numbers were in the double digits, but not out of the teens. "Go on."

"You wanting me again isn't something I understand. I thought you might be disappointed."

"Hardly. Nothing about that night disappointed. I can't get it out of my mind." He made a mental note to take care of her, even if they never touched again.

"Really? It seemed we exhausted everything that night, all those positions. I mean…" She broke off as her face heated. "We were talking about how to move forward as friends."

"And we went on a tangent, but it's one I think we should follow." Michael's tone was serious as a nail driving into a block of wood. He shifted on the couch, moving forward, closer to her. "We'd barely scratched the surface that night."

Ione again clutched her knees. "There's more? I mean, I know there is. I've read books. I've seen pictures. But I didn't think that applied to us or one-night stands."

"Ione, what am I going to do with you?" Michael braved moving to sit next to her. He still allowed plenty of space. "Do you know how refreshing I find you? How wonderful that is?"

Lips he longed to kiss puckered. "You mean I'm not as socially savvy as your other women."

"And thank God for that." He held out his hand and was glad when she took it. His fingers laced around hers in reassurance. "You're a breath of fresh air. And there are no other women. Not since you. I'll tell you that a hundred times until you believe it."

"I meant the ones before."

His fingertips memorized the texture of her palm, tracing circles in the center. "I didn't come out of a sealed bag so, yes, I have a checkered past I'm not proud of, one that is still far less than the media pretends. Let me be honest. Our night together lives rent-free in my brain. I've often wondered how you were. Seeing you walk into Kaiser's today was like Christmas, and I'm not ashamed to admit it."

* * *

As Michael made another circle, Ione's palm quivered. Adrenaline pumped through her veins. Already her heart raced faster than it did when she maneuvered a kayak through whitewater rapids and felt the cold spray on her face as her stomach launched itself up and down. She had to remember three things. One, he was an expert in the art of seduction. Two, she worked for him. She had to do a job. Three…there was a third one, but she had no idea what it was again. Friends? Was that it? They were talking about being friends. But the sensations created by his simple touch said that would be impossible. But he'd also mentioned that maybe it could be the start of something more.

She tempered any sense of joy and removed her hand from his. She had no idea what more meant. Did it matter?

"Ione, come back from wherever you are. I'm sorry if I'm handling things badly." He bent low, as if to peer up at her.

"I don't know how to handle this, either, especially as I thought…" She couldn't say it.

"You thought I was a playboy who used you." He gave her hand a quick, reassuring squeeze before releasing her. "It's okay."

"I didn't have 'be a notch on a bedpost' on my bucket list," she admitted. "Then again, I hadn't researched one-night stands before I asked you for one, either. I just knew I wanted you."

"I did ask for your contact information. That was important to me."

"Only so that I could tell you if I was pregnant or not.

Which I wasn't." And never planned to be, either. Not with her mother's ovarian cancer history and the fact she might have the genetic markers. She should get tested, but her family had enough to deal with. Then there was the fact that she two months shy of thirty-five, that magical number where children born to older mothers had higher risks of complications or birth defects. Science called those pregnancies geriatric, an insulting term if there ever was one.

"I would have supported you if you had been pregnant," Michael said, filling the silence.

His brother Liam had gotten his now-wife pregnant during a one-night stand. "That's good to know, but clearly unnecessary. What we need to do is discuss how we act in public. We lost sight of that somewhere in this conversation."

He gave her a one-shouldered shrug. "It's simple. We stick to the truth, that you helped me with the bats. I remembered your earlier assistance, so I brought you back for the eagles, especially when I found out you worked for the company Liam suggested."

"I do have some ideas for your eagle problem. I was doing some research and…"

A knock sounded, and she rose to answer the door, Michael behind her. Since the desk was full, the server set the tray on the coffee table. Michael signed the slip and began removing the lids. The food looked delicious. "Tell me your ideas for the eagles while we eat," he suggested.

She could do that. They had been rehashing the same information and getting nowhere. She cut her sandwich in half. "I did some research…" She paused as a random thought struck her. "I say that a lot, don't I?"

"I find it one of your adorable quirks. Go on."

She had adorable quirks? She considered that as Michael uncorked the bottle of white wine he'd ordered. He gestured with a glass. "Would you like some?"

"Sure. Thank you." One glass wouldn't hurt or make her lose her wits. "In regards to the eagles, there was a similar situation during the construction of Highway 54 in Camden and Miller Counties."

"West of here," Michael clarified.

"Yes. They found a nest like yours, with two adults and two nestlings, along the new road alignment." She ate a French fry. Unlike some hotels, the Grand's kitchen had perfected the art of room service. She had hot and fresh food. "The nest was found along the new highway, about fifty feet into the trees. The Missouri Department of Transportation worked with the US Fish and Wildlife Service and the Missouri Department of Conservation to remove the nest once the birds left for the season. I'm proposing that Clayton Holdings use the same solution. However, removing the nest will require approval from the feds."

"But what about the eagles? Don't they return to the area?" Michael asked. "Their nest will be gone."

"Eagles do return to the same area, but when they find the nest gone, they'll search for a new place to build. If your construction has started when they return, they'll recognize that and instead relocate in what they consider a safe place, which will be nearby. They might even settle in the acreage you set aside for the bats. The would be ideal, since that's protected because of all the covenants. As for the loss of the nest, Missouri has a lot of severe weather. It's not as if the eagles come back and think 'oh, humans took out our nest.' It just won't be there. They know what to do and will rebuild."

"I like the idea."

"The eaglets have a fledging period of ten-to-twelve weeks, which is when their wings become large enough for flight. Even after that, young eagles will often stay near the nest for several weeks since their parents will feed and protect them while they work on their flying and hunting skills. Once that's done, they'll move on, and we should be okay to move forward."

"But what specific month?" Michael asked. "My father will want a time frame. By my calculations, it's the start of July before they'll leave."

"Actually, it can be anywhere from now until the end of July. I've been watching your live cam and I want to see the area myself. We should be able to secure the permit to remove the nest. From the video feed, the nest appears approximately five feet in diameter and three feet deep, which means it's average size. I expect the Department of Conservation will want to keep the nest for research purposes, as they did with the other one. And they'll secure a permit to use the feathers for genetic fingerprinting and future study. That's an extra step, but a necessary one to ensure all parties are happy."

"I never knew dealing with eagles was this involved," Michael said as he lifted one of his own fries and brought it to his mouth. "I should have, I guess, after the bats."

Ione washed her bite of her roast-beef sandwich down with a sip of wine. "With some exceptions, but not in our case, a federal permit is always required to possess eagle feathers. The conservation department will acquire that. My job is to act in your interests while also protecting wildlife. I find the middle ground to make everyone happy. Tell me more about the building project while I eat. It's my understanding that repositioning one of the golf course greens is the issue."

As Michael began telling her about the new hotel and the PGA-worthy eighteen-hole golf course, Ione sipped her wine and ate her sandwich, salad and fries. Michael grew animated as he spoke, providing her with additional insight into what made him tick. The night they met they'd avoided getting too personal. Today they dug deeper, which she appreciated. He'd surprised her and she found herself glad of it.

"I'm impressed with everything you've done," she told him when he finished. "You're good at your job."

"Thank you." From the way he quickly dipped his head for a moment, she swore her compliment had mattered. But when he met her gaze, he seemed resigned. "I wish my father felt that way. It was my brother who insisted we use solar and geothermal for power. We're working on being carbon-neutral."

"A noble goal. But why isn't your dad impressed? I am." It was important he know that.

Michael refilled his wineglass. "Because running Clayton Hotels was never supposed to be my job. Edmund, that's my oldest brother, was to take over and become CEO. When he decided to travel with his fiancée instead, I was tapped to run the hotels and Liam got the wineries. I'm not sure how my father even chose who got what. Maybe he flipped a coin."

Michael shook his head, sending his hair onto his

forehead. He shoved it back. "Edmund hasn't returned, and despite the fact we've passed the year mark in our new roles, my dad remains CEO. The night you met me, I was at loose ends. Still am, honestly. I'm not certain if running hotels is what I truly want to be doing." He added a sheepish grin and an eye roll. "Which makes me sound like a poor little rich boy who has daddy issues."

"I don't see you as that." Ione unwrapped the plate of cookies and withdrew a chocolate-chip one. The cookie was soft and crumbly when she broke it in half. "What do you want to be doing?"

"Do you know no one has ever asked me that? They only see me as a playboy who can't keep his pants zipped, not as someone who has an MBA. It's tiring."

"I can imagine." Ione set her empty plate aside. "Halloween weekend I was trying to put my past behind me. Seems like we were both trying to do the same thing when we met, which is why I'm giving you the benefit of the doubt."

"I appreciate that." Michael removed the used dishes, loaded the tray and put it outside. He sat next to her, his leg inches from hers. "That weekend I found you. And then you were gone. And afterward I figured it was time to do something positive."

Ione resisted shifting and closing the gap between them. "I like to think people can change. Even if we don't know whether that's nature or nurture, or if it's preordained or not, it's worth a try."

To occupy fingers that itched to touch him, she snagged the remaining half of the decadent cookie she'd eaten earlier. As she wrapped her mouth around it, she noticed that his eyes darkened. His fingers clenched the stem of the wineglass. That's what desire looked like, she realized. He wasn't lying when he said he wanted her. She gestured with her free hand. "Take a cookie. Eat something, especially as you ordered them. I don't want them to go to waste."

When he bit into a cookie, Ione regretted her encouragement. Watching his mouth move made her libido flare to life. No, that word was far too basic, too elemental for the yearning flowing through her veins. Her longing ran deeper, to a foreign place she didn't understand. As if her thoughts were written on her face, he set down the cookie. "Ione."

Even she could read these social clues, especially as he made no attempt to hide his feelings. A thrill shot through her, pinballing from her heart to her head.

"Michael." His name danced on her tongue. Where were the words to say? "We can't" or "We shouldn't"? Those words died in a mouth whetted with a fortifying sip of wine. She wanted him, plain and simple.

He eased to the edge of the couch, but made no attempt to stand. "I should go."

"If you must." Disappointment consumed her, until she noted he made no effort to leave. She set down her empty wineglass. If she looked at her choices like an environmental problem, logically, she had a multitude of reasons to say no and no good ones to say yes. Touching him would complicate matters. Nothing long-term could come from giving in to temptation. What was that saying her mom had always used? Play with fire and get burned. Michael was molten lava. Safe when viewed from a distance. But also with the power to cause destruction and the ability to change everything in its path. He'd already changed her.

She bit her lip as her body, mind and spirit fought the war. She and Michael were a conflict of interest, and she knew better. But she wanted to know what would happen if she took him to her bed again. What happened the morning after a second-night stand? Was there such a thing? A protocol? And by even thinking about it, what did that make her? Or who?

"What happens if I want you to stay?" she asked. "What happens then?"

Ione waited with bated breath as Michael considered her question. "Do you want me to stay?" he asked. "Because you've thrown me for a complete loop. I want you like no other woman. So if you're asking me to stay, tell me." He pushed his water bottle and his glass toward the center of the coffee table. "Is that what you want? Another night?"

"It's what I'm trying to decide. I'm risking a lot. I feel like a moth uncontrollably drawn to a porch light and praying it's not a bug zapper. Not that bugs pray. But all the reasons line up in the this-is-wrong column. But yet it feels so right."

"I will never intentionally hurt you. Knowing you need things spelled out, I'm trying to find the best words. I'm not going to be some dirty little secret you only tell your friend Cordelia. I feel something here. I want to pursue this. And if we pursue this, that means tomorrow is just another morning after. Same for the next night and the next day. We take it one day at a time, like I said earlier. We enjoy each other until we want other things or we don't want to pursue a relationship anymore. And if we choose to exit the relationship, we have civil conversations about it. So as for a second night, why stop there?"

"But is that a relationship?"

"It is. You should know that I don't share. If you and I are sleeping together, we are monogamous until one of us ends it. That's one definition of a relationship. As for your conflict of interest, I see none if we set guidelines."

"I agree. That's acceptable. Sex only. No other feelings. I have a lot going on. I need to find a place for Cordelia's wedding. I need to help my mother with her cancer treatments. My sister is getting divorced. I have a job to do."

She sipped some water, but it did little to cool her throat. "I know you don't like feeling like a dirty little secret, but no one, and I mean no one, can know we're having sex. Those are my conditions. Not as long as I'm working for you. And, yes, I know it's my company you hired, so don't call me out on a technicality. So while we may hang out, we are not lovers in public."

As she stated the words, for the first time in her life a sense of feminine power overtook her and washed away any rational thoughts she might hold dear. She mentally warned herself not to read too much into the giddy feeling traveling through her. One more night, or many more nights, likely meant nothing to him. Despite Michael's half-year celibacy, he was still a former playboy with far more experience than she'd ever have. He'd dated beautiful women, the kind that turned heads and wore designer clothes from head to toe. Whatever Ione shared with him would be temporary. She would be wise to remember that. He was also younger. Eventually he'd want to marry, and when he did, he'd want someone closer to his age and his social class.

If she remained in control of her emotions, she could handle when things ended. She'd handled Henry, hadn't she? And that had been an embarrassing humiliation. "Those are my terms."

"I accept."

Michael didn't like the words he'd spoken, but he'd said them, anyway. If he wanted to be with Ione, he had no other choice but to accept whatever crumbs she'd give him. It was an odd place to be. While she might think she was a moth attracted to a light, he was caught in a Death Star tractor beam that had clutched him months ago. She might believe her decision was some form of negotiation, but it was one-sided. She held all the cards. He wanted her too much to say no. "I can live with those conditions."

Even if he couldn't. Hadn't he told her all or nothing? Yet here he was agreeing to everything, and praying she'd change her mind.

"But I do have some terms of my own. I want us to make a commitment to communicating and talking things out. If you don't want to be with me, I want you to use words and tell me. I'll do the same. If one of us decides we don't want to sleep together again…" He couldn't imagine it would be him. "Well, that's that."

"Okay." She wiggled a finger at him.

His eyebrow lifted. "What's that mean?"

"Have I done it wrong? It's the come-here gesture, right? Did you want to shake on it?"

"No. It's this." He crooked a finger and beckoned her. "Tell me what you want, Ione."

"Now that we've established the ground rules, I want you to show me what more there is. The below the surface. What you alluded to earlier."

"Ah." It didn't matter one bit that he hadn't gotten resolution, or any answers as to why she was underneath his skin. It didn't matter, anyway. Not when she crooked her finger.

"There you go. I was just waiting for the right sign." He brought his lips to hers for a kiss before telling her the words that sealed his fate and ceded her the power to hurt him.

"This," he said, kissing her again, "is the beginning. The best is yet to come."

Chapter Six

"This is where you'll be meeting. Do you need help setting up the tech? Mr. Clayton said I was to provide you with anything you need."

Ione smiled reassuringly at the young administrative assistant who appeared slightly nervous. Ione didn't blame her. She felt the same, especially since she'd learned Michael's father was definitely coming. "I can set up. I appreciate you showing me everything. Thank you."

Ione glanced around the oversize Clayton Hotels conference room. After working most of the morning in her suite at the Grand, she'd driven to the corporate offices, located in downtown Beaumont. Alone in the room, she unpacked her laptop and attached it to the room's top-of-the-line presentation connections. Hard to believe that five hours ago she'd been kissing Michael goodbye and sending him away from her suite before the sun rose. That was after they had swapped phone numbers, sending those obligatory this-is-Ione and Michael texts.

Her phone pinged with another from him: See you soon. You got this.

Her heart jumped. She bit her lip and shoved aside her

excitement. The text meant nothing. He would attend the meeting alongside some other executives. The text was akin to the same sort her other colleagues would send, like Marty, whom she'd worked with in West Virginia. He was married, with three kids, and their work relationship was nothing but professional. She'd never said anything personal to Marty, unlike Michael. And her stomach never flipped around Marty like it did when Michael slid into a chair at the conference table.

The morning meeting was with the Clayton executives. Michael occupied the front right spot, which meant he was directly in her line of sight. She kept her expression neutral as she greeted everyone and resisted the urge to hold Michael's hand a second longer than necessary. After a night spent in his arms, his presence didn't unnerve her, but his proximity created a sense of hyperawareness, as if the room's electrons zinged directly from his orbit to hers. Thankfully, no one else registered the strange undercurrent sending heat waves from head to toe.

She roused her computer. Long ago she'd taught herself how to control her emotions and remain impassive. Once she'd learned her brain was wired differently, she'd spent years refining her coping mechanisms. She could drill down to the basics and compartmentalize. She hyperfocused and addressed things objectively, even when doing so seemed impossible. Knowing Michael liked her ideas for relocating the eagles did make things easier. Plus, she'd done dozens of these presentations. She wouldn't let him down, or herself.

Still, she caught herself trying to look at Michael more than any of the others. She fought a subconscious that wanted to fixate on how good he looked in his dark blue dress slacks and crisp white cotton shirt. Sans tie, he'd left the top two buttons undone. Her presentation, which should be her sole focus, seemed like foreplay for something later. She clicked on her final slide. "Once Clayton Holdings gives its approval, I'll present the formalized plan to the state and local officials."

Ione glanced at her watch as she sat. She'd left plenty of time for questions.

"Which you'll do this afternoon," Wyatt Jones said.

Ione managed not to gasp. She'd thought she had at least a day or two for additional preparations, which included visiting the nest. "This afternoon?"

"Yes. Mr. Clayton told me to schedule our first meeting with federal officials for this afternoon," Wyatt said. The senior environmental team leader glanced across the table at Michael. "Your father moved it forward."

"And clearly he had other things come up before he could inform me," Michael said, the set of his lips indicating his displeasure. No wonder he'd made that statement about his father the night before. But he took the change in stride. "Thank you," he told Wyatt.

Michael glanced at the leaders of various construction and environmental teams who were present. "I'll assume he'll be at the afternoon meeting. Thank you for rescheduling it. My father values efficiency, and since our time is limited and he chose not to attend this morning, I'm sure we can agree that we'll run with Dr. Scott's plan to remove the nest and force the eagles to relocate. It's a good idea, especially as there is a precedent in the state for this type of action. Unless there's anything else, I'll fill my father in on our discussion when I meet with him next."

Michael rose, signaling that the meeting was over. "Dr. Scott, will you stay behind a moment?"

"Certainly." She ignored the way her adrenaline spiked and watched as the rest of the room filed out, minus Michael's sister. Eva, who remained seated, was typing something on her phone. When she finished, she glanced up.

"Sorry. I was making some notes." Eva pocketed the phone, stood and came toward Ione. Eva might be petite, but she made up for it in poise, grace and innate confidence, all things Ione had had to learn. Eva thrust her hand forward. "Eva Clayton. VP of PR. It's nice to meet you, Dr. Scott. Michael told me that you're the one we have to thank for his idea about the bats."

"We discussed it last Halloween when we met at Kaiser's. We were the only people over twenty-two in the place and found ourselves sitting next to each other at the bar."

A slight hyperbole, but one that stuck close to the truth she and Michael had decided to tell. But there was a slight speculation to Eva's gaze that made Ione nervous, as if the younger woman could see through the holes in the story. "My friend owns it, so I was there after finishing a tour. Well, I was leading a ghost tour. My sister owns a tour company and I was filling in for her." Ione clamped her mouth shut as she realized she was oversharing, one of her biggest flaws aside from her bluntness.

"Ah, well, fortunately for us you were in the right place at the right time." Eva turned to her brother. "Don't be long. Dad will want to know what was decided and you know how he hates it if we're late for lunch."

"Be right there. I was going to show Ione the office we set up for her."

Eva paused, one foot in the room and one foot out. Her assessing expression had returned. "Ione? I thought your name was Hermione."

"I use Hermione for work purposes as it's my given name. My friends call me Ione." As nerves clanged in loud warning, Ione gave what she hoped was a friendly yet professional smile. She and Michael had already failed their first test in keeping people from speculating. "Feel free to call me that as well."

"Okay, I will." After an arch of an eyebrow that she directed toward her brother, Eva disappeared through the doorway.

"Your presentation went well," Michael said when they were alone. "We've put you one level down. It's easier if we take the stairs than wait for the elevator."

"Gets my steps in, too." She never had gotten around to taking that walk last night, opting for Michael-involved activities instead. After unhooking her laptop, she followed him a short distance to the end of the hall. They entered the stairwell, went down a half level and paused on the landing.

He slid a loose strand of hair behind her ear. "Hey, there. How are you holding up? You did great."

"Fine." Pleased by his compliment, she decided not to bring up his sister's contemplative gaze. "The presentation went well."

"I never had any doubts. But I meant how are you doing after last night? We didn't get much sleep. I know I'm tired, but it was worth it."

"Oh." Her face heated as she remembered his touch.

When he'd said *more*, he'd meant it. The second time around had been even better than the first, even more amazing.

He traced a finger along her cheek. "Do you know how much I want to kiss you right now?"

"You can't. And don't worry. I'll be at my best after lunch, even if I wasn't expecting to meet with the federal and state officials so soon. I wanted to see the nest first. Get my bearings."

"Of course, you'll be at your best. I have complete confidence in you. And changing plans is what my father does. He makes everyone jump when he says jump. He doesn't even have the courtesy to say anything. He just acts."

"That must be annoying."

"An understatement if there ever was one. I'll try to give him a piece of my mind when I see him later, the key word being *try*. And I have no doubt you'll knock things out of the park. You wowed me in there."

His sincere compliments sent tingles to her toes. "How about we meet for dinner later tonight? Will that work?" he asked. "Until then…"

Michael moved closer, but before he could kiss her, a door opened somewhere above them and he stepped back and morphed into professional mode. "Let me show you your office."

On the next landing, he held the door open. This floor housed the environmental department, and most people worked at various oversize cubicles in the middle of the large space. He led her to one of the offices lining the perimeter. "I hope you like it. This is yours."

"Oh, this is perfect." The eight-by-ten room had a

glass interior wall with working blinds and a view facing the cubicles. She had an actual door that closed and two solid walls between her office and the ones on either side. A large window dominated the exterior wall, letting in light so that the space was well-lit. Complete with two bookcases, a nondescript gray laminate desk and black mesh rolling chair, and a landline phone, the room reminded Ione of one of her professor's offices in college. Basic, utilitarian and ready to be occupied. It was more than she had at Good-4 Environmental.

Michael gave an offhand wave. "Feel free to decorate however you want. I want you to feel at home. I have to go to meet my father and sister for lunch, but I'll try to touch base with you before the meeting with the feds. If not, I'll see you in the conference room at two p.m."

Before Ione could reply, a young red-haired woman appeared in the doorway. Michael introduced them. "Hey, Carolyn, I'd like you to meet Ione. Ione, this is Carolyn. She's the lead administrative assistant for the environmental team, so that means she's your go-to person, She'll help you get settled and onboard you with whatever you need. If you have a question, Carolyn will have the answer. Don't hesitate to ask."

"Nice to meet you," Ione told her as Michael slid past without a backward glance.

Fifteen minutes later, Ione had a filled calendar containing meetings with various project managers, the landscape architect and the building architects. "Thanks," she told Carolyn when they were done.

"You're not overloaded?"

She'd never admit it if she was. Ione shook her head.

"I've been through much worse. You were thorough, which I appreciate. Makes my job so much easier."

"Good to hear. I'll check on you in a little bit." With a smile, the administrative assistant left.

Several hours later, Ione was satisfied with her work. She'd put the final touches on her updated presentation for the state and federal officials, and she was doing a final run-through when she sensed someone in the doorway. Most likely Michael, she assumed, as he'd said he'd stop by and it was after the lunch meeting he'd had with his father.

Ione grabbed a napkin and wiped her mouth—she'd been munching on a bag of potato chips and the chicken-salad sandwich that Carolyn had had the first-floor cafeteria send up. Used to doing everything for herself, Ione was grateful, especially as the last thing Ione wanted was her stomach rumbling during the presentation. She made a mental note to tell Michael how Carolyn had been indispensable.

"Hey there," Ione said, raising her head to greet the person in the doorway. "How did your…" The rest of the words died on her tongue. It wasn't Michael standing there.

"Hello, Hermione," ex-boyfriend Henry Summers said, giving her the wide, toothy grin that had once weakened her knees. "Fancy seeing you here. Imagine my surprise when I saw your name in my email."

"Henry." Ione's stomach began a series of somersaults. She shoved her hands into her lap. "What are you doing here?"

As Henry peeled himself off the doorjamb—how long had he been lounging there, studying her?—she already knew. He was the federal official. To calm her nerves, she ran her hands over her blue skirt, as if to smooth out wayward wrinkles she couldn't even see since they were hidden by her desktop.

"I've clearly surprised you, which wasn't my intention. I know you don't like surprises, but you were working so intently I figured I'd wait until you looked up. Looks like we'll be working together again."

The beautiful smile she'd once found charming lessened, and brown eyes that matched his floppy, sun-streaked hair lifted as he awaited her reply. She couldn't find one, so she said, "Oh. I see. I didn't realize you'd moved."

"Why should you? We lost touch."

Like Michael, the gods had unfairly gifted Henry with good genetics. Maybe that's what had first attracted her to him—he reminded her of a youthful Andrew Mc-Carthy, with those wide eyes, straight, slightly upturned nose and full lips. Henry's attention had been flattering. After being a social outcast in high school and college, here was a desirable man wanting her. His interest had been a novel fantasy and had served as proof she was normal. Until he'd trashed her ego, she'd truly believed he'd cared for her. As Henry straightened off the door-jamb, her skin prickled, but not with the giddy awareness she got when being near Michael. She found that odd and another point in Michael's favor.

"Do come in," she offered since Henry was already halfway to her desk. Three inches shorter than she was, what he didn't have in height, Henry made up for in swagger. When he walked into a bar, women turned their heads and flocked in his direction. He sauntered into her office full of a confidence she wished she could bottle, so that she could project the same.

Charm overflowed as he dropped into the chair on the other side of the desk. "I can't believe no one told you I transferred to the Midwest region. I'm based in Bloomington. Minnesota, not Illinois."

"Congrats." Her stomach was trying to churn butter and she willed it to stop.

"When I saw your name associated with the project, I couldn't believe it and had to come myself. How have you been?"

Her hands safely out of sight, she made two fists, released them and worked for an upbeat, light tone. "Fantastic. I just finished a project in West Virginia and am happy to be back home." Her public-speaking-course instructor would be proud of how composed Ione sounded.

He tapped a finger on her desk. "That's right, you're from Beaumont. Your hometown is rather small, isn't it?"

Ione's hackles rose. "Clayton Holdings has propelled the region to national prominence and Good-4 Environmental is pleased to have partnered with them on multiple projects. And we're just forty-five minutes from St. Louis. You should visit the Gateway Arch while you're here."

He held up his both of his hands, palms toward her. "Relax. I didn't mean to offend. Missouri has some great wetlands that I've been exploring." He gave her another grin before his gaze shifted. "When did you arrive?"

She managed an airy, lighthearted wave toward the empty walls and lack of personal touches. "Last night. Haven't had a chance to settle in. You?"

He shifted again, the movement drawing her attention to his slim yet muscular figure. "I've been in the state about two weeks. I'm following through on some department initiatives. Drove in last night from Columbia. I've been working out of the Missouri Ecological Services field office there."

"Ah." As the shock of seeing him wore off, keeping her tone light came easier. "I expect some of them will be at the meeting later."

Dressed in business casual, Henry brushed a piece of lint from his long-sleeved polo. "Not as many as you'd think. There's one maternity leave and one paternity leave. Since I was already here, the assistant regional director asked me to lead this project."

"You're the lead on this?" The food she'd eaten threatened a reappearance and Ione took a fortifying sip of water. "You're the decision maker."

That smile he'd once bestowed so freely came easily again. "Yes. That's usually what being lead means. I saw this as an opportunity for us to become reacquainted. We didn't part on good terms, and I'm sorry for that."

"You're sorry?" Was she going to keep parroting his words? She had to get it together. No way could she believe this. Henry was apologizing and the lead on her project. It could not be happening, but it was. Cordelia would call it a nasty turn of fate.

"Of course, I'm sorry. I was under a lot of pressure. I handled things poorly, especially after I'd told you I loved you. I never meant to hurt you."

"Thank you for saying that." What did one do after one's ex came back and apologized? She had no clue. Maybe buy a lottery ticket? See if pigs were flying?

Henry pressed two forefingers onto her desk, as if wiping away an imaginary spot. "I was jerk. Anyway, this project will let us work together again, even if we are on opposite sides. We were good at that once, yes?"

Long before they'd complicated things by dating, they'd made a good team. But Henry had had ambitions to move up the career ladder, which had often come at Ione's expense. She realized that fact in hindsight. Clearly, he'd climbed several rungs if he'd moved to a different office. "We were. Once."

"Exactly." Henry tapped a finger on the desk. "And I miss that. And we both want what's best for the eagles. That's one thing I always respected about you. You always work for the best outcome for wildlife. I hope that hasn't changed."

"Of course not." That's what made her so good at her job and why she loved her career. She truly believed there had to be a way for man's progress to work in harmony with nature. Once mankind realized its own actions were the variable, the future was possible. It boiled down to finding an equitable solution beneficial for all parties. In this case, the Clayton family and the eagles. Henry was an unexpected complication, both personally and professionally. She'd been in meetings with him. Knew how he operated.

"Good. I'm glad we're on the same page." Ione didn't correct him as Henry moved his fingers back into his lap. "I've always liked you, Ione. I hope you can forgive me because I've missed you. Let's do dinner tonight, shall we? I want to hear more about the eagles. I've seen the nest on the live cam. We think it's a new nesting pair, which means everyone in the field office is excited. Have you seen the nest or the birds yet?"

He'd sent several things by her rapid-fire, including

an invite to dinner and the fact he'd researched the nest. She focused on that. "I'd planned on visiting the nest tomorrow. I thought that I'd have the chance this afternoon until the CEO moved the meeting timetable forward. He's worried about another construction delay."

"That means we'll see it together. Like old times. We can chat over dinner tonight." Henry's pleased expression gave Ione pause. She couldn't do dinner with Henry. That was too much, too soon, when she didn't even know how she felt about him being here or what he'd said.

Carolyn's appearance in the doorway saved Ione from having to reply or find an excuse. If Carolyn was surprised by the presence Ione's guest, her professional expression never changed. Ione's opinion of the young woman rose even further. "Sorry for the interruption, Dr. Scott. I wanted to let you know that Mr. Clayton's lunch meeting ran late but he's on his way. Mr. Summers, the rest of your party has arrived. If you'd follow me?"

"Certainly." Henry stood and leaned over the desk to shake Ione's hand, which he held a beat longer than necessary. Ione resisted the urge to wipe her hand on her skirt. Unlike Michael's heated touch, Henry's was clammy. He said, "Looking forward to seeing what you've come up with," then exited.

After he left, Ione took a few deep breaths. She moved her mouth in a circle, trying to loosen frozen muscles. Henry had apologized. He'd said he was jerk. He'd said he missed her. What was that about? His whole demeanor had been so unlike the man she'd dated and once thought she'd loved. She pinched herself to be sure this wasn't a dream. Nope. She was wide-awake. The day, which had started with Michael in her bed, had turned even more surreal.

"How's it going?"

Ione's hand flew to her chest. She gazed up at Michael, whose head tilted to study her.

"Are you okay?"

"Oh. Hey. Hi."

"What's going on?" Michael eased inside the office and shut the door behind him. "You look like you saw a ghost, and if memory serves, you don't believe in those."

"You startled me, that's all." She prayed he hadn't seen her trying to de-stress. She wrangled her composure and prayed her best attempt to reassure him hadn't failed. "I'm ready to go. Let me grab my laptop."

The *M* between his eyebrows revealed his skepticism. "If you're sure that's it."

"Of course. What else would it be?" Ione forced herself to relax, lest she worry him further. While they'd promised each other they wouldn't lie, would a little stretch of the truth hurt here? After dealing with her ex, she needed things to be as impersonal and compartmentalized as possible, especially since seeing Henry had been a shock to her system. As for Michael, she worked for him. The vertical blinds on the wall overlooking the cubicles remained open, so anyone looking through the glass would see two colleagues discussing a project, nothing more. Ione busied herself by packing her belongings. She glanced at her watch. If they left now, they'd be early.

She lifted her bag onto her shoulder and hoped she came across as a competent professional. "I'm ready."

Before he held open the door, Michael's fingers lightly

grazed hers as she went by. "Like I said in my earlier text, you got this."

"Thanks. I appreciate your confidence." She needed it, Ione realized, as she and Michael entered the conference room. A dozen people milled about. She immediately recognized Eva, Wyatt and the few people from earlier. A man who appeared to be an older version of Michael chatted with Wyatt and Eva. This must be Michael's father, Edmund Clayton Jr. He'd appeared this time.

Henry stood in the opposite corner, a glass of water in his hand as he chatted with two other men. At least she hadn't been blindsided by Henry's appearance. She also knew better than to let her guard down.

"Shall we?" Michael lowered himself into a chair. Following his lead, people sat around the U-shaped table. Ione sat directly across from Michael and Eva sat to her right. Once he was satisfied he commanded the room, Michael began speaking.

"Thank you everyone for being here. I'm Michael Clayton and on behalf of the entire Clayton family, we're looking forward to this partnership between Clayton Holdings, the US Fish and Wildlife Service and the Missouri Department of Conservation. Let's take a moment to introduce ourselves, shall we?"

"I'm Edmund Clayton Junior, CEO," Michael's father said. Next came Wyatt Jones and several other Clayton Holdings executives. The woman who represented the state department of conservation told them to call her Beverly Jean. The perky platinum blonde also told them her interests lay in acquiring a permit to keep the nest and a collection of feathers for DNA sampling. Ione had expected that, and because of the state's interests, she tentatively considered Beverly Jean an ally. What Ione didn't expect was her own reaction to the way Beverly Jean eyed Michael, as if he was something she also wanted to add to her collection.

"I'm Henry Summers," Ione's ex said, drawing her attention in his direction. His introduction of the two others from the US Fish and Wildlife Service established Henry as the lead, as he'd indicated earlier. He'd be the one signing off on the plan. That meant that without his approval, nothing could happen. No progress would be made. The golf-course construction would not start and she would have failed.

Michael recognized this as well, and at his subtle nod, Ione rose. She'd handled dozens of meetings similar to this one, worked too hard to overcome her social anxiety to let Henry's presence, and his earlier declarations, distract her.

"Welcome. I'm Dr. Hermione Scott, and I'm the Good-4 Environmental consultant representing Clayton Holdings in this endeavor. I'm delighted to make your acquaintances and look forward to working with all of you. Let me first explain the problem and show you the solution I'm proposing. Once we all understand the scope, we can work in the best interests of all parties, including our nation's precious national symbol."

Confident in her content, especially with the changes she'd made from the morning, Ione went through her presentation. When she finished, she controlled her expression and the immediate drop of her stomach as Henry raised two fingers.

"Dr. Scott, correct me if I'm wrong, but the precedent

that you cited, that was for highway construction, not a golf course, correct? Or did I misunderstand?"

Ione's stomach clenched. Henry had lobbed an easy, softball question. The next one would be like a dart aiming for the bull's-eye. "Yes. It was for the construction of Highway 54."

Henry leaned forward and tapped his fingers together, reminding her of one of those cartoon villains hatching a plan. "Thank you for that clarification."

He paused a beat too long, a technique she'd seen him do more times than she could count. Here came the hammer.

"Dr. Scott, wouldn't you agree that it would be rather dangerous if we allowed for eagles' nests to be removed anytime someone or some corporation wants to build something? A highway is a civic project, a necessary evil designed for the good of many. This construction, this removal of a nest, is being done for the convenience of a private enterprise, for a private use of the land."

If he thought she'd cave, Henry had another think coming. She directed her answer at him. "Thank you, Mr. Summers. That's an excellent point for consideration."

"Henry," he corrected.

"Henry." Ione gave him a smile that didn't reach her eyes. "However, while an excellent point, it's important to remember that while Clayton Holdings is a private entity, court cases have given corporations rights that are often considered inalienable and once reserved for citizens. Clayton Holdings has abided by all tenets of the law, but even better, Clayton Holdings, represented by those in the room, has worked for the betterment not only of their profit margins, but for the betterment of the county, region and state. The company's commitment to the environment is unparalleled. As for the grounds, all are welcome to book a stay here. They can come and eat at the restaurant. Book time on the course. It's not someone putting in a swimming pool for their own personal purpose or cutting down protected trees to ensure a better view."

Henry glanced around, as if assessing the mood of the others in the room. The woman from the conservation department frowned. "To accommodate the endangered bats, Clayton Holdings moved the project," Henry said. "Why won't that work here?"

Ah, there was the gauntlet, and Ione was prepared. "Clayton Holdings has already modified the scope and scale of this specific project by donating land to the conservation department, as Ms. Neeley can attest. But because of that generous donation, the land that remains is limited. If you look at the plans, Clayton is already planning for additional woodlands as a buffer between the course and the conservation area, where we're expecting the eagles to rebuild once they return. Since Clayton is playing host to a PGA golf tournament, which will bring national attention to this region, bringing Beaumont additional growth and revenue, timing is of the essence to build a course worthy of the PGA."

"Clayton Holdings is the majority landowner in the entirety of Beaumont County. It has a conflict of interest with its need for profit," Henry pointed out.

He was sparring with her, like they'd done when they'd debated politics or projects over dinner.

"While Clayton Holdings may own the majority of the land, the region's geographical features do not allow for building in all locations. The use of the land in the county is limited, which works in Mother Nature's favor as this means much of the land will remain in its natural state. Removing the nest once the eagles have migrated is the best solution. We expect the eagles will return to the area to nest, as eagles like to return to where they hatched and fledged. And unlike with the highway, the eagles who return won't be in danger of being hit by cars."

"Just golf balls," Henry added, earning mild chuckles from his coworkers. "Or are you planning on installing one of those ugly nets like those used at a driving range?"

Ione's lips thinned and her gaze narrowed. Besides her own irritation at such a ridiculous assumption, she sensed the proverbial steam rising from Michael's father. However, Mr. Clayton hadn't remained a powerful CEO by losing his temper and interjecting his opinions. His company had hired her for that.

"While there are stories of waterfowl like geese being hit by golf balls, the designers factored these concerns into their revised plans. Removing the nest will actually make it safer for the eagles. And why would you suggest we would be considering using a net when the purpose is to harmonize with nature? That seems to be an unnecessary assumption of a company that has done everything right and is pioneering the way in sustainable, carbon-neutral hospitality."

Ione's cool tone had Henry straightening. She'd shocked him with her blunt reply. She pushed forward before he could defend himself. "I believe when you stopped by my office earlier, you said you wanted to see the nest? Perhaps once you see the topography and the actual distance from the edge of the course to where we're hoping the eagles resettle, you'll know that even a PGA champion wouldn't be hitting a ball that far."

Heads at the table swiveled from watching Ione to waiting for Henry's reaction. Henry gave her a noncommittal nod. "Thank you for clarifying. I look forward to you showing me the nest and the site plans so that you and I can work together on this and find a solution."

Henry had said everything in a politically correct, neutral tone, but Ione sensed an unspoken undercurrent. It wasn't the one that she'd felt when they used to work together, but at the same time, his thoughtful gaze held something different. Not pride or respect, but something that indicated he saw her differently, in a better light. Although something still bothered her.

She risked glancing at Michael. His fingers twisted the pen he was holding, sending it round and round like a slow, spinning top. His gaze had fixated on Henry, sizing him up.

Ione regrouped. "As this is our first meeting and time is of the essence, why don't we schedule a visit to the site? Say, tomorrow? Once we've visited the location, we can reconvene, discuss the details and go from there. I'm certain Clayton Holdings will easily prove that moving the nest will not harm the eagles. As firm believers in protecting the environment and with a demonstrated commitment to doing so, Clayton Holdings wants to work to continue to grow the state's population of eagles, which was nearly thirty-seven hundred statewide last winter. Correct, Beverly Jean?"

"Yes. We're proud of the fact we've had a hand in that." The conservation agent gave Ione a smile. She spoke in a mid-Missouri drawl, an accent different from that of even Beaumont. This was the state where half the population said, "Missou-ree," and the other half said, "Missour-uh."

"And we plan to be good citizens and to continue that work." Ione gave the group a brief, friendly smile. "Thank you for coming today. At this time, I believe we have our next steps. Mr. Clayton?"

Ione ceded the floor to Michael, and she sat down harder than expected. Michael stood, his face schooled into professional neutral. "Thank you, Dr. Scott. We do have our next steps." He turned to the federal and state officials. "Before everyone leaves, let's get things set up for the site visit."

"I'd like to be present," Beverly Jean said. "Eagles are a passion project of mine."

"I don't think that's necessary." Henry shook his head for added emphasis. "To protect the integrity of the site, it's better to have fewer people in the area. Reports have reached me that because of the live stream, random people are venturing onto the property. Correct?"

"We've hired additional security to protect the site," Wyatt Jones said. "We will let no harm come to the birds."

Henry closed the folder containing a copy of Ione's presentation. "It's best if Dr. Scott and I visit alone and report back. Once the birds migrate, anyone can visit. If there's anything left to see." He directed this last comment at Beverly Jean. "Until that time, we need to protect the eagles from as much human interference as possible. Wouldn't you agree with my assessment, Dr. Scott?" Henry didn't give her time to answer. "As for finding the nest, it's not like you and I don't know how to use a compass. We did work together once, so I know you're quite capable."

She was more than capable, but when Ione's mouth dropped open, no words came out. Michael regained control of the meeting. "Great. I'm glad that's settled. Dr. Scott and Mr. Summers can visit the nest and report back. As Dr. Scott has other projects she's working on for Clayton Holdings, before you leave let's have Carolyn can set up a time that works best for both of you. Thanks, everyone, for coming. Carolyn will send out an email with a recap of today's meeting. Carolyn?"

Ione's assistant waved from the doorway, once again showing her impeccable timing.

Michael's father and sister exited first, followed by the Clayton execs. Ione wanted to flee, but curiosity about what Henry might say to Michael kept her rooted in her seat. Michael also hadn't dismissed her. He paid the company that signed her checks, and she did want to spend some time debriefing with him.

"It was nice meeting you, Michael," Henry said, his casual use of Michael's name another way of establishing his authority in this situation and putting each man on the same level. Henry shook Michael's hand as he went by, then tilted his head her direction. "Ione."

"Henry." She watched as Carolyn led the feds from the conference room.

Michael returned to his chair and swiveled so he faced Ione. A line of worry etched into his brow and joined his deep frown. "What was that? You worked with him?" he asked.

"Yes, on several projects while I was with the US Fish

and Wildlife Service." Not a lie. "I didn't know he'd be the one overseeing our project." Also not a lie. She was still reeling from the impact.

"I would have thought that you knowing someone was a benefit, but that meeting did not inspire my father with confidence."

He left the "or me" unspoken, for which Ione was grateful. She could tell. No need to hear him speak the words. She was frazzled by this entire situation, too. But it could be controlled and she would make it happen. At least she hoped she could. "I can understand your father's and your frustration, but let me reassure you that the meeting actually went very well."

No way would she let Michael know the interaction with Henry had shaken her. They'd always been on the same side before, so she hadn't been ready for him to needle her, especially so soon after asking her forgiveness. Perhaps he hadn't changed as much as she'd initially thought. Henry always had an agenda, but she had no clue what it could be.

"Working to donate the land was much simpler," Michael admitted.

"Of course, because that was the state and they were getting things for free. In my experience, both as a consultant and from when I was a government official, federal agencies don't rubber stamp things willy-nilly. There's a process. Hurdles to jump. The first meeting is an introductory meeting. Your father may not like that he didn't get the results he wanted today, but this relocation will get done. Once Henry visits the site, he'll be able to look at the plans and approve them."

"And you've worked with him so you know this."

"We were in the same region when I worked for the service. His first concern is for the wildlife. He's a fair man." That much she could truthfully say. Adding that Henry was always a bit of an arrogant jerk wouldn't help—she'd seen her ex in many meetings like this. And she certainly wouldn't tell Michael that Henry was her ex.

Ione's phone pinged with a text, the specific chime she'd never changed, indicating the message was from Henry. Strange how after all this time she still recognized the sound and felt the jolt of adrenaline seeing his text message gave her. She faltered. Was the adrenaline the same type as what had rushed through her when she basked in the heat of Michael's gaze? Or was it more like when she'd scored an ace in volleyball? Better if she concentrated on Michael, a man whose mere presence caused little prickles of awareness to run along her spine and needy pressure to pulse between her legs.

"If you're sure," he said.

"I am. Once we do a site visit, we'll meet with the architects and address all of Henry's concerns. I'm confident that once he sees everything and understands Clayton's perspective, we can get your project back on schedule."

"What I'm hearing is that I should trust you."

"Yes." As Michael held her gaze, Ione resisted the childish urge to cross her fingers. She would get this deal done. Business came first. She wouldn't disappoint him in this.

Michael sighed. "I mean, I have so far."

Even with her stunted social skills, Ione could read between the lines of his double entendre. She'd said nothing about their affair, unlike many of the women who'd given exclusives to the media. Either that, or they'd made their own TikToks.

"I'm on your side here. Even without our history, I want what's best for you. I take it that's not always been the case."

"No, and that matters. I want this time to be different. I'm glad you're different. I wish…" Michael appeared flustered, as if the heat had kicked on. "Never mind. Shall we go? We can talk later. We're still meeting for dinner, right?"

"No. Sorry. I need to work on your project. Please understand."

She probably did need to see her ex and figure out what he wanted. She'd also work to convince Henry that her way in regard to the eagles was the correct way. Besides, as much as she wanted to spend time with Michael, it could be dangerous. Already she missed his kisses. Wanted to live out the fantasy by getting up, locking the door and having her way with him on the conference table. And she wasn't the type of girl who had fantasies, much less indulged them. "Can we rain check? We could meet for breakfast and talk."

"Sure." He stretched his arm as if ready to grab the pen sitting on the table but he didn't pick it up. He opened his phone instead. "I'll meet you at the Grand's restaurant, say at eight? I have to check in with the manager about something else, so I'll be onsite."

"Perfect." Ione plugged the appointment into her phone and noted she had three unread texts, one from Henry's number and two from a number she didn't recognize. "I have it down."

"Good. Same." Michael pocketed his phone, rose and stepped toward her.

"Ione?" Carolyn's voice arrived before she did, and Michael stepped back. Carolyn came in and if she thought anything was odd, her face remained a mask. "Here you are. I've been looking for you. I had some questions and you weren't answering your texts. I need to make the schedule. I have the times Mr. Summers suggested, but wanted to confirm with you first."

Well, that explained the unknown number. "That sounds reasonable. Thank you." Ione gave Michael a brief smile as she scurried toward the door. "Mr. Clayton."

"Good chat," Michael said simply. "I'll add breakfast to our shared calendar."

"Perfect." As she followed Carolyn at a speedy pace, Ione told herself she had to remember what was important: work. Ione had a job to do and a bonus on the line that would pay for her mother's treatment. That was her priority. Along with finding a new venue for Cordelia's wedding and helping her find a solution to her business problems.

Michael? Henry? Both were distractions she needed to push aside and forget about. Even if one was as sexy as sin, with lovemaking that rocked her world, while the other one had once told her he loved her and hinted he might want to marry her someday, and now he was asking for forgiveness and saying he'd been a jerk.

She needed to compartmentalize and banish them from her thoughts immediately.

Chapter Seven

Since one should never show up empty-handed, Michael juggled a bottle of wine in one hand while he rang Eva's doorbell with the other. Then he used his key and entered.

"I thought you had dinner plans?" Eva called from her condo's kitchen. Wiping her hands on a towel, she rounded the corner. "Your text came out of the blue. And don't forget your shoes."

Michael slipped off his shoes. With an all-white house whose pops of colors came from the artwork, decorative pieces and knickknacks, Eva had a thing about dirt. Michael slid his feet into the custom slippers she'd had made for him. "Things changed and I didn't want to eat alone."

He set the bottle of wine on the kitchen counter.

"You're lucky I was home and could whip something up."

"I told you I would have brought takeout." Michael withdrew two glasses from the cabinet. "I appreciate you letting me crash your night in. Thanks." He uncorked the bottle he'd snagged from one of their wineries on the way over, poured two glasses and handed her one.

"Well, you seemed out of sorts. Still do."

He took a sip of the Jamestown Norton. "A little. I had plans and then nope, canceled. And when they were, I realized that being canceled on mattered more than I would have liked."

Eva lifted the lid on a saucepan. Steam rose and droplets dripped back into the sauce. "Her loss is my gain. I'm assuming it's a she. It normally is, especially given your agitated state. That's the only time I see you like this. Although, honestly, you seem more invested that usual. It can't be Amy can it?"

"And you'd be correct on all counts, including that it's not Amy." Michael relocated to one of the counter stools lining the large kitchen island. Eva had ten-foot ceilings on the first floor, which provided a feeling of spaciousness. He toasted her with his glass. "Besides, who doesn't love a home-cooked meal. You had me at spaghetti and wine."

Eva poured wine from a different bottle into the saucepan. She stirred and replaced the lid. "Don't get your hopes up. The sauce is from a jar and the noodles are from a box, but I did empty an extra can of diced tomatoes into the mix and sautéed the meat myself. And I added red wine. Lots of wine. What you're seeing is the full extent of my cooking skills."

"More than I've got." He stretched his feet over another the rung of another stool. "And whatever you've cooked will be better than microwaving or eating out. At this point even the Grand's food is getting old. I've had every item on the menu far too many times. We need to add some seasonal options along with the evening specials. Shake up the offerings some. We don't want people to get bored."

"That's a good idea. You should get on that."

"Adding it to the list." Michael set a reminder on his phone.

Eva turned off the stovetop and strained the cooked noodles into a colander. She added the pasta into the pan holding the sauce and began stirring it together. "Grab some bowls. We're not standing on ceremony tonight, so make yourself useful. There's grated cheese in the fridge."

Michael brought over bowls, silverware and the bag of cheese. He held up the clear plastic bag with shredded Parmesan inside. "Fancy."

"I got it from the Grand's kitchen. The chef's trying out a new proprietary blend. When you see her next, you can let her know what you think. Now, eat up"

They ate at the island, discussing the day's meeting and their father's disappointment in between bites. Eva's spaghetti hit the spot and he let his sister know. "What did Ione say after I left?" Eva asked.

Michael swirled some noodles around his fork. "That we shouldn't worry, that the federal agencies never tip their hands this early. There's a process. She says this posturing is normal."

"That's makes sense. So she's confident things will go our way."

His mouth full, Michael nodded.

"Good. Dad will feel much better hearing that. He's never hosted a PGA tournament before at any of our properties, so the fact we're hosting one in Beaumont will be a crowning achievement. It'll be his swan song, his way to go out on top."

"It's a lot of pressure to make sure things are perfect." Ready to change the subject, he aimed his fork at the plate and gestured. "You can cook for me any day."

Eva laughed. "The Caesar salad is a kit from the produce section and the bread is from a bag in the bakery aisle. You have a kitchen. You could make something like this yourself. All you have to do is go shopping and fill up your refrigerator with things besides water, beer and condiments. There's even this thing called the internet that shows you how to do it."

Michael shuddered. "No thank you. I hate cooking, which is why I don't know how to do it."

"You don't know how to do it because we always had nannies or chefs," Eva corrected. "Don't try to lie to me. I was there."

Did Ione enjoy cooking? He figured she must enjoy some part of it, especially as she went camping and had to prepare her own meals. Or did she eat those MRE things, like they did in the army? He gave another shudder.

Eva noticed. "Okay, that second body twitch is not because I suggested you actually cook something and venture into the foreign land called a supermarket. What's up?"

"I've been to a supermarket," Michael defended. "And if you want to know, I was thinking of something Ione said about camping. Like with a tent. Not the RV kind. Who does that?"

"Clearly Ione. And lots of people enjoy camping or we wouldn't have had to include so many restrictions when we donated the land to the conservation department. If we hadn't, we could have had a campground instead of a nature preserve next to us." Eva studied him. "How did you segue to camping from cooking?"

"I don't know." He'd hoped to see Ione tonight and instead he had to wait until 8:00 a.m. He was the one normally needing space, so this out-of-sorts feeling was more foreign than the supermarket.

"Why don't you tell me what's going on between you two?"

"Nothing."

Eva shook her head. She'd always been good at reading each of her brothers. "Try again. Because you went from cooking to camping, and that's a big leap. She might be visiting the eagles' nest tomorrow, but that doesn't require a tent. You could get there yourself, but you'd have to wear bug spray. Smell like the deep woods so the critters don't attack."

Michael wrinkled his nose. "Nothing's going on." He washed the lie down with a sip of red wine. "And that sounds awful."

"You need to get out more. Do you some good. And you know, after Edmund and Liam, not much gets past me, not like it did when I was in my teens. And unlike our brothers, at least you haven't slept with her and not known who she was…" Eva's voice trailed off as he dipped his head. "Michael! She's been in town one day. How could you? Seriously? That's fast even for you. I can't believe this. This fast after Amy? That's a record even for you."

"You hated Amy."

"True. She wasn't right for you. But our consultant?"

He set his fork on the table and wiped his lips. "I didn't know she was our consultant. We met last Halloween. After Liam's wedding. I knew her name, but not that she was Hermione. I met *I-own-ee*. Not *Her-my-oh-knee*." He emphasized and expressed each syllable. "It's an easy mistake to make. I didn't know they were the same person until she showed up."

"Like at the meeting?"

"No, when we ran into each other at Kaiser's last night after her friend told her I was there. Kaiser's is where we first met after Liam's wedding. I hadn't gone there since Halloween. By then, she knew who I was, as she researches all her clients. So the joke was on me when she walked in."

Eva set her fork down. "Let me confirm what things happened between you."

"Which time?" Michael felt his face heat as his sister threw up her hands. "Halloween weekend or last night?"

"Michael! You never change. I cannot believe you."

"Stop raking me over the coals. You don't get to accuse me of not changing. I never even kissed Amy. Ione is the only person I've slept with since October. Minus last night, I don't even know when I'll see her again like that. We work together. We had plans, but she canceled. We have to be professional. Her insistence. I said one day at a time. She pushed me off to a breakfast meeting tomorrow."

"Please. When has that stopped you? Don't you remember Samantha?" Eva's eyes performed their classic roll.

"I was a college student. We were summer interns with fixed exit dates. And I was young and stupid."

"Proven by when she started talking about quitting college and staying with you forever. Thankfully, her parents talked her out of throwing her future away. You got lucky. Clayton Holdings got lucky. What does Ione think of your reputation?"

"Well, she canceled on me tonight if that answers your question. And she doesn't want anyone to know anything happened between us. She hates my past as much as I do."

"Smart woman. I knew my first impressions were positive for a reason."

He fingered the cloth napkin. "She's much smarter than me. I'll admit, it's a bit unnerving how she sees me. Besides her friend Cordelia, she wants no one to know about us. I feel like a dirty little secret and I don't like it."

Sensing he wasn't done, Eva clamped her mouth shut and held her tongue. Michael knew it was difficult.

"Ione wants to keep work at work. Minus me helping her find a venue for her best friend's wedding, personal is personal. So, no, to circle back to your original questions, she doesn't want to be tainted by my reputation. She's told me as much."

"I respect that," Eva said. "She's a woman in a man's world. If I hadn't seen you in an unguarded moment a few minutes ago, I never would have put two and two together. Her reputation will take far more of hit than yours if people learn the two of you have had sex. It could jeopardize everything, especially for her. You'll just make the online gossips happy they can vilify you again."

Michael sighed. "Saying it was sex makes what we did sound cheap, and it wasn't."

Eva's right eyebrow mimicked the Gateway Arch standing tall on the St. Louis riverfront. "You *like* her. Like actually care about her."

"Very much," Michael admitted. "If that's what the fact I can't stop thinking of her means. She's special. I was totally enamored by her when we met. We talked so honestly. It was great. She didn't know I was Michael Clayton, the notorious playboy, until she accepted the job to come here and started doing her due diligence."

"But she slept with you again, anyway." Eva shook her head. "Because you can't help yourself."

"I am pretty irresistible." Michael's poor attempt at a joke fell flat, even to his own ears. But no way was he going to tell Eva that Ione had propositioned him.

Eva scowled. "What am I going to do with you?"

He'd asked Ione the same question, and she him. Michael shifted, the stool starting to be uncomfortable. Or maybe it was simply his sister's probing. "Nothing. She and I will be professional and do these two projects, and when they're done, most likely she'll go on her merry way, leaving me behind, and we'll both move on. I'd like more, but it's up to her."

"Huh." Eva stared at him, as if trying to figure something out. Either that or he had something on his face. He used his napkin just in case.

"Did I get it?"

"What? No. Your face is fine. I find it interesting that you've fallen for the one woman you can't have. That you're letting her be in the driver's seat of your relationship. And that she likes camping, which means she's *so* not your normal type."

He scoffed. "I haven't fallen for anyone. I turned over

a new leaf. I'm being discriminating, something you've all wanted."

"Of course, that's the reason." Eva's annoying eye roll emphasized her sarcasm. "You may have thought you were on a new path, at least until she walked back into your life. One thing's for sure. She's got you in knots and it's amusing me that you've fallen for someone whose idea of fun is tromping through the woods. Especially when your idea of taking a hike is walking a golf course with your clubs in tow."

"Gee, thanks."

Eva, to her credit, managed not to laugh at him. She swallowed the one snicker attempting to escape. "All things Liam loves that you hate."

"Yeah, she'd be perfect for him, if he hadn't met Lexi first."

"Well, you know what they say about opposites attracting. Who would have thought our brother would marry a famous pop star? Maybe you've met your match. At least Ione and Liam will have something to talk about at Christmastime."

"Doubtful she'll be around that long. Doubtful she's my match." Michael didn't like saying the words. They felt wrong on his tongue, tasted like sandpaper. The words made him feel as if a missing part of him had been located, but that it was still out of his grasp. "But I admit I would like the opportunity to find out. She makes me feel things. It's different with her. And you know I don't say that."

"You don't. I never thought I'd see a day when a woman was under your skin." Eva rose and began to clear away the empty plates. "You've never had to deal with rejection. You're the one leaving them behind. Even what's her name. The one who set you up at the costume ball and still would have taken you back."

Michael hadn't thought of her in months. "You mean Rachel. And is it wrong to want more? To want a soul mate? I mean, who wouldn't? Whoever she is, I don't want to be seen as a checkbook or as a means to having the good life."

"You think Ione won't want you once work is over and done?"

"You saw her today. She's all about the job. Building her career. I can't fault her for that." Michael had dealt with people prioritizing work his entire life, starting with his father and brothers. Even Eva let nothing stop her from doing the work she loved. He changed the subject. "Speaking of, what's your read on the fed? Henry Summers."

"Besides the fact that he's good-looking in that late-eighties way?"

"I hadn't noticed that."

"Liar." Eva chortled. "That poor conservation rep couldn't keep her eyes off him or you. Henry Summers has Liam's outdoorsy vibe. All those lean muscles and floppy hair. I wouldn't kick him out if he showed up on my doorstep."

"And you say I'm the playboy?" Although the reality was that Eva had few notches on her bedpost. She talked a good game, but was far too guarded.

"I don't think Henry's going to be an issue. Ione handled him well. He's here to do his job. Once we convince him his job is to help us relocate the eagles, he'll sign off and get things done. Ione is right on that." Eva

moved pans into the dishwasher. "Oh, wait. I just realized something. They seemed to know each other. He
called her Ione."

"They've worked together before. Ione told me that
after the meeting."

Eva grinned. "Oh, now I see the problem. You're
afraid he's into her. Classic. You've got competition. The
great Michael, whom all women fall for, has a rival." She
tilted her head and studied him. "He's as good-looking as
you are. It's different, of course, sort of like the Aveng-
ers movies. You know, Bucky Barnes? He's much more
my type than Captain America or Iron Man."

Michael raked a hand though his hair. "It's not a competition. I don't want anything to get in the way of this
project. We're dealing with Dad, remember? The sooner
this goes forward, the sooner I can figure out whether I
want to stay or go. I promised I'd see this project through
when I agreed to extend the original year."

Eva folded her arms. "Sure. That's the whole reason
you're all hot and bothered. I wish Edmund and Liam were
here to see how flustered you are. It's finally your turn.
I'd revel in your discomfort, but I'm too nice of a sister."

"You're imagining things that aren't there," Michael
insisted. If he told the lie enough times surely it would
become true, or at least be believed. Wasn't that how the
reiteration effect worked?

"Keep telling yourself that," Eva said. "I minored in
psychology. You can't pull one over on me. The bottom
line is that you like her, you want her and she's going to
keep you at arm's length while going to see some birds
with another guy. And you don't like it."

"I don't," he admitted. "But they're professionals."

Although he'd sensed a vibe, an undercurrent that had rubbed him wrong. He couldn't quite put his finger on what it was.

Eva shut the dishwasher door. "Oh, how the mighty have fallen. And by that I mean you."

"I haven't fallen. That makes it seem like I'm in grade school. I don't fall for women."

Eva snickered, then sobered. "There's always a first time. This might be it. What if she's the one?"

Perhaps it was the first time, because his emotions were jumbled like never before. Michael couldn't stop thinking of her, even after he and Eva settled in to stream the latest action-adventure thriller. As the bullets began to fly, he decided Ione had him off-kilter. He shouldn't be wondering what she was doing or wanting to text her. He shoved his hand into the bowl of buttery microwave popcorn rather than reach for his phone.

The media had declared him shallow. Perhaps he should live up to that. Digging into why he was on edge over a woman he'd slept with twice felt unwise. Sure, he liked her. Wanted to get to know her. But he knew you didn't get everything you wanted. If he attributed his current funk to his father's pressure to perform in the VP role, all could be explained away. No woman had ever gotten under his skin like Ione had. Last night, he'd said to take things one day at a time. Wondered if she'd be a woman he could love. Had experienced bliss in her arms. Today, he questioned if he'd been too hasty. Maybe blinded by infatuation.

"Stop thinking," Eva commanded.

Turning his attention back to the movie, Michael did his best.

* * *

In the end, Ione didn't see Henry, either. When her sister, Arwen, called, Ione immediately put her family first. When she texted him that she had a family emergency, Henry had sent her one word in response: fine.

Based on past history, she expected she'd irritated him, but seeing her mother for the first time in several months was the priority. Arwen had cooked a beef stew and her mother had seemed brighter and more with it during dinner. Ione had loved seeing her niece and nephew. Much to their delight, she'd lost when playing their favorite video game. They'd watched a film before calling it a night. She and her mom hadn't discussed her treatment, especially as Ione had sensed that tonight that was the way her mother wanted it. She knew her mother's brave face, knew the front she put on for the kids. Her mom had insisted that she would be at Cordelia's bridal shower.

"Earth to Ione." Michael waved a hand in front of her face. "What's got you so deep in thought? Were you thinking about today's meetings?"

"Huh?" Ione glanced up from the waffle she was currently cutting into. She and Michael sat across from each other in the restaurant of the Beaumont Grand. To a casual observer, the breakfast appeared to be a business meeting. However, to anyone watching closely, they might have noticed some strain between the two, especially since aside from ordering and a few pleasantries, they hadn't spoken much. Ione didn't know if that was a good thing or not. "Sorry. No. I didn't get much work done. I went to see my mom."

"How is she feeling? Any updates on the cancer?"

Ione sighed. "We didn't discuss the fact that I know she's not responding to the latest treatment as well as her doctors would like. But she seemed in good spirits. We'll talk later this week. There's a new drug the doctors want to try, but we have some hoops to jump through first." Like finances, Ione didn't add.

Michael's perfect eyebrows knit into a straight line. "That sucks. Can I do anything?"

"It's kind of you to offer, but if you miraculously find me a wedding venue, that's all I need."

"I've got that meeting today while you're out hiking. Although there's a bulldozed trail through the farm field. You'll be in an UTV most of the way."

"Almost seems unfair to poor Henry," Ione said, earning her a chuckle.

"It's not like we're in the wilderness. Clayton Holdings has dedicated three hundred and fifty acres for this course, a size on par with Augusta National. Not all of those are maintained turf."

"I have no idea what goes into designing a golf course." She'd researched it, but there were knowledge gaps that she expected the designer to fill in once she met him.

"You'd be amazed. Besides the greens, there's tee boxes, fairways, roughs, water features, paths, woods. There's also infrastructure such as the clubhouse, cart garages and other outbuildings, like rest areas and snack shacks."

"I had no idea."

"Think of it as being like a sports stadium where both participant and spectator amenities each need to be considered. Not to mention employees. This course will have sixty full-time groundskeepers. Then there's the executive managers and various auxiliary staff. To support this, we're working on making our course one of the most ecofriendly in the country, utilizing all the latest building and management techniques. People don't realize how sustainable golf courses can be. Liam wants us to become a certified Audubon sanctuary, like Osprey Point."

Ione made mental notes. "I'll add these details to my research. Once I see the plans, that's something I can help you with. We'll make this course the talk of the town, and, of course, the PGA."

"Thank you. My father will be thrilled." Michael sipped his orange juice, and Ione had to wrench her gaze from his lips. "Is it okay if I tell you that I missed you last night? I'll admit I worried when you said you were going to be working that you might have met up with Henry or something, and I'm not allowed to be jealous. I have no claim over you. But I'm glad you saw your mom. I went to Eva's."

"How is she?"

"Great. I should tell you that I told Eva about us."

"Oh." That was a surprise. Ione didn't know how she felt about his revelation.

"I know you wanted to keep things secret, and she will. She's my best friend. Yours knows about us. I figured telling my sister was fair."

She couldn't find fault in that logic. "I have an ally and now, so do you."

He bit into his last piece of bacon. Ione tried not to focus on Michael's mouth and how he even made chewing seem sexy. He had those perfect lips, the full and plump kind that reminded her of a ripe berry. She pushed her empty plate forward and checked her messages. She couldn't allow herself to become distracted.

"Henry texted that he's on his way. He should be here in twenty minutes." Seeing Michael was finished, Ione stood and reached for her backpack. Inside she had sunscreen, bug spray, water, a compass, GPS, a topographical map, a first-aid kit, binoculars and other essentials, including two extra pairs of socks, a jacket, phone cords and a power bank. She'd dressed in layers, including hiking pants, a ribbed cotton tank, a long-sleeved shirt, a windbreaker and her favorite pair of boots. She'd tamed her hair and secured a hat atop her head. Because the journey was short, she didn't need trekking poles, so she'd left those in her hotel room.

Michael left the signed folio for the server and followed her to the lobby. As she made for the restroom, he told her he'd have the valet bring the UTV around. When Ione returned to the lobby and stepped under the Grand's portico, a blue Polaris General waited. Clayton Holdings had spared no expense on the side-by-side. "You can drive one of these, right?"

She grinned. "Of course."

"Then you'll have to take me for a ride later. Show me what this can do. It's so new I doubt anyone's had it out long."

Ione laughed. "You clearly don't value your life if you're wanting me to go off-road."

Michael's wide smile was like golden honey flowing over a honey dripper—positively decadent. "I thrive on danger."

"You do, huh? Can't wait until you prove it." Proud

of herself for a flirty comeback, Ione basked in his attention.

His subsequent wink rewarded her and provided a tiny thrill. Then he turned serious. "Take care of yourself today, okay? Text me when you get back."

A car arrived and Henry stepped out of the driver's side. His glance flickered, assessing the situation. "Ione. Michael. I didn't expect you to be here."

"We had a breakfast meeting. And I wanted Ione to have access to the UTV. She'll drive you to the site. After all, she works for us. Ione, you ready?" Even Ione recognized the smoothness in Michael's tone as the two men shook hands. He'd put Henry in his place, let him know whose turf he was on. Henry would ride as Ione's passenger. The man might control the fate of the permit, but Michael was only willing to bend so far.

Ione palmed the keys. Michael had given her a modicum of control by making her the driver, giving her a way to level out Henry's natural superiority. She gave her ex a pointed stare. "Shall we go?"

"Certainly." As Henry rounded the front of the UTV, Ione mouthed "thank you" at Michael. A slight dip of his chin indicated he'd seen her. Ione climbed inside. Besides the tip-out front windshield, today the vehicle was configured to be open to the air. After strapping in and ensuring Henry had done the same, Ione started the ignition and she and Henry were off.

She'd memorized the path last night. They soon passed the stakes driven into the open ground, marking the location for the new hotel. Beyond those, she easily found the construction tracks that led toward the future golf course. The UTV easily handled the ruts and bumps as it crossed the former farm field. Not even ten minutes later, she made another turn and parked at the edge of the forest.

"These trees are mostly American elms, many of which have Dutch elm disease." She pointed. "You can see the yellow leaves. And those over there are brown. This entire thicket is mostly elms, and that's why Clayton's arborist scheduled them for removal." Ione stepped out of the UTV and sprayed on insect repellant. Henry did the same. Already Missouri's three species of ticks were making their appearance, and the last thing Ione wanted was to be at risk for Lyme disease or Rocky Mountain spotted fever, especially as Missouri ranked in the top five states for the latter.

"Look!" Henry exclaimed, pointing upward. An eagle flew low with a fish clutched in its talons. The bird disappeared into the thicket in front of them.

Ione consulted the map to find the outline of an earlier footpath. Created by those who'd found the nest and those who'd placed the live-stream camera, the path was still visible. Mother Nature always needed some time to make things new again. After adjusting her backpack and checking her hat was secure, Ione stepped forward. "This way."

They spotted the nest about fifty feet high in a cottonwood tree. While they couldn't look directly into the nest, they could hear bird noises coming from above. "Look at the size of that," Henry said. "I can see why Beverly Jean wants it. It's bigger than the video makes it seem."

"It is impressive."

Ione unfolded the project map. After studying it, she

pointed to the trees. "You can see from the markings there how many elms are dying. This entire area needs to be removed so that the disease can be contained. The plan is to level it to provide an overshot area around the ninth hole, keeping the few larger maples and oaks intact."

She walked farther into the woods until she located a stake. She pointed to where they were on the plans. "The tree removal stops here. The rest of this will remain forest."

"So the justification for clear-cutting this is the fact that the majority of the trees are elms."

"Almost all, including many in the understory. You know as well as I do that there's precedent for removing diseased trees. The National Park Service removed the ash trees on the Gateway Arch grounds and replaced them with London planes. In fact, because so many parts of St. Louis replaced their ash trees with elms, they're now having to replace trees again. All thanks to the emerald ash borer, an invasive species of green beetle. Removing the trees is the only way to stop its spread."

"Yes, I know it's a beetle," Henry told her, but his tone didn't seem as condescending as it had in the past. "Is this the end of the Clayton property, or is this the end of the acreage allocated to the golf course?"

Ione checked the plans. "Clayton property extends another three linear acres, but they plan to leave that as natural green space, as it abuts the conservation area. Here." She handed him a corner of the map.

"Got it." Henry studied the map, then the terrain, before giving her a grin. "This is like old times."

"Uh-huh," Ione mumbled noncommittally as Henry

had turned to peer in another direction. When he let go of the map so he could stride off, she instinctively caught it.

"I want to walk the perimeter. Coming?"

As if she had a choice. "Sure." Ione grabbed her backpack and followed him through the woods. Henry made one-sided conversation as they cut through the underbrush, telling her about people they'd once known. With a few exceptions, most of the people she'd worked with in Alaska had moved on to different locations and positions. She brushed off a tick that had landed on her sleeve, then glanced at her watch. They'd hiked into the conservation area, almost all the way to the edge of the bluff overlooking the river. "Are you ready to go back, or is there more?"

"What, are you starting to suspect I just wanted to get you out in nature?" He grinned, but his smile didn't affect her as it once had. Still, there were some tugs at her heartstrings.

"No, I'm in nature all the time. I don't sit behind a desk all day. I did get to hike some of the Appalachian Trail on my last job. But time is of the essence for our reports."

He stretched his arms out, as if measuring the distance between a huge oak and the maple beside it. "You need to lighten up. Inhale. Exhale. This land is gorgeous. I've never been in this part of the country before. I wanted to see for myself that the eagles would have enough privacy. You know how they screech at humans when they feel threatened by them. I don't want anything to happen to them. Remember that guy who pled guilty to killing thousands of birds in Western Montana? Sold their feathers on the black market and bragged about it. I hope he rots in prison and that the fine bankrupts him."

Ione had read about that. "The Claytons are committed to ensuring the birds' survival. Liam Clayton wants the golf course to become a certified Audubon sanctuary. I told Michael that I'd help research that."

"How long are you here for?" Light filtered through the tree canopy, creating a dappled glow on the forest floor.

"Unknown. I'm consulting on pollinator projects for the area Clayton wineries. It's another of Liam's pet projects."

"Sounds like you and Liam would get along." Henry began to lead the way back.

"Maybe. He's married to Lexi Henderson. They're currently in Nepal, opening a school."

"What about Michael Clayton? He gave me the evil eye today." Henry moved a low branch out of the way and made sure it didn't snap back as Ione passed through. "He's good-looking, I'll grant you that. But I know you, Ione. He's not your type. I doubt he's ever been outdoors, much less gone hiking or camping."

"I'm certain that's true." But Michael had other attributes that made up for his lack of outdoor skills. A breeze filtered through the trees, making the understory rustle and the temperature drop.

"Are we supposed to get rain?" Henry asked.

They'd arrived back to the area of woods near the nest. "I don't think so. I checked the forecast."

But Missouri was like that, Ione knew. In the spring, pop-up thunderstorms could occur, with some even turning severe. As long as the weekend of Cordelia's shower went off without a hitch, everything would be fine.

Ione raised her binoculars and gazed upward, seeing slivers of blue-gray sky through the trees that had leafed out early. "Hey, there," she said, stopping.

Realizing she wasn't behind him, Henry turned to follow her gaze.

An eagle rested on a thick tree branch, its white head, yellow eyes and beak visible. "Look at you," Ione whispered. "And who might you be? Mom or Dad?" Although female birds were often larger, unless the male was right next to the female it was impossible to tell which was which. "Doesn't matter. You are gorgeous." She made an unspoken promise she'd keep the bird safe.

"Ione? You've seen plenty of raptors," Henry declared.

True. But that didn't mean every encounter, especially one this close in the wild, wasn't impressive. Mother Nature might often be violent, but she had her beautiful, still moments as well. The word *spiritual* came to mind, but Ione dismissed it.

"Ione, our timetable? The one you set?" Henry reminded her.

"Give me a moment." After taking a photo, Ione eased her way through the brush until she joined Henry where he impatiently waited.

He brushed a twig from her sleeve before they began walking. "You'll need to do a full tick check when you get back. I'll help if you want."

The wind gust saved her from replying. "Looks like the weather forecasters got it wrong. Storm's coming. We need to hurry."

They climbed into the UTV as the first fat raindrop landed. Thankfully, the sky didn't open fully until they were under the Grand's portico. When Ione gave the keys to the valet, he said, "Mr. Clayton said I'm to store this for your use. You tell me which vehicle you want and I'll bring it around. And if you want this one enclosed."

"He gave you a UTV?" Henry watched as the valet drove off.

"To use. I'll be all over the property working on the pollinator projects as well." Ione tried not to read too much into Michael's actions. He was simply being efficient, like with the suite.

"Maybe I should take a turn at the private sector." He shook his head. "Nah. I like being one of the good guys instead of a corporate shill."

Ione resented the implication that she'd sold out. She would still be working for the service had her and Henry's relationship not gone sour. And she was one of the good guys, too. It was the reason she worked for Good-4 and not somewhere else. But she said nothing as the valet returned with Henry's government-issued vehicle.

Henry paused before climbing in. "Shall we retry dinner tonight? Discuss our findings, among other things? I'm meeting my crew for a late lunch."

Beyond the portico the rain came in heavy sheets. Ione had no desire to go out in this weather. She glanced at her watch and ignored her growling stomach.

"I'll text you later once I've done a little work. I'm going to review our findings, check my email and update the Claytons. I'll see what I can do, but you should know that my priority is my family while I'm here."

"Tell your mother I hope she feels better soon." As if

aware of the observant hotel staff, Henry leaned closer. "I enjoyed working with you today. Touch base with me later."

"I will." She would, if only to give him an answer one way or the other. But right now, she had a meeting to cancel and ticks to check for. Alone.

The pouring rain hadn't subsided by late afternoon, prompting the National Weather Service to issue a flash-flood warning for Beaumont County. The Missouri River wasn't yet a concern. It was the multitude of small tributaries that, while mere trickles most days, turned into raging torrents, making low bridges and low roadways impassible. A mere foot of rushing water could wash a car away, with two feet enough to float SUVs and pickup trucks. Michael knew well the turn-around-and-don't-drown campaign. Clayton Holdings had donated money to the county so it could install warning signs on public roadways.

High and dry, Michael sat in his fifth-floor office. One of the taller buildings at the edge of historic Beaumont, he had a view of the storm water flowing across the road toward the Missouri River. He finished an email, pressed Send and leaned back. Minus an email update, he hadn't heard from Ione since her visit to the nest.

The valet had alerted him when she'd returned, which had been far later than he'd expected. She'd canceled the meeting since she had no new information and advised her team she'd be working from the hotel. Smart, as it was raining buckets.

That didn't mean he'd stopped questioning his sanity for caring so much. First, when he hadn't heard from her, he'd wondered exactly how long a visit to the nest took. Then he'd checked with the valet to see if she'd returned, rationalizing his actions as a way to ensure her safety. Then he'd read her email and tried to figure out if there was anything he'd missed between the lines. Knowing Ione, she'd simply meant what she said, which in itself was a new experience. Most women he'd slept with played games, with every text or email a form of innuendo. Unable to apply previous experience to his current dilemma had sent him down another rabbit hole, disturbing his concentration throughout one meeting and two projects.

His computer dinged, and he opened the email that arrived from one of the wedding coordinators. He clicked on it—any diversion or crisis was a way to stop thinking of Ione and the blatant interest in Henry's eyes. Michael scanned the email and dialed the number at the bottom. "Phyllis, it's Michael."

The voice of Chateau's top wedding planner came through crystal clear. Phyllis handled all their celebrity clients and had made the move from Portland to Beaumont to oversee the entire wedding-events department.

"I've got good news for you. The Chateau can handle the wedding and reception. My plan is that we'll hold your friend's reception in a tent, as the ballroom and terrace are booked for the entire day, but if they agree to use the French garden and change the time of their ceremony, I can make it work. We also have a suite I can set aside for the bridal party, which we can clean and redo during the ceremony so that the married couple can have it for their wedding night."

"Phyllis, you're a goddess."

She laughed. "Remember that at bonus time. I have her contact information along with their contract. Do you want me to contact the bride? Knowing what you wanted, I prioritized this one."

"Yes. Do it. And whatever the price differential, charge it back to my discretionary account. Whatever you do, do not give the bride or anyone else the information that Clayton Hotels is subsidizing anything. As far as anyone in the wedding party knows, it costs the same here as at the Annex."

"I can do that. Discretion is my middle name. I'll email you with what she says."

"She's going to say yes." Michael glanced at his watch. "Tell you what, give me an hour and then contact the bride. I want to do something first."

"Whatever you say. You're the boss."

"That I am." Michael grinned as he put down the receiver. Finally some good news. Relief and excitement rushed through him. He had no qualms about going out into this weather. Time to go tell the maid of honor he'd performed her requested miracle.

Chapter Eight

One of Ione's vices, if it could be called that, was her love of music, which was why she had 875 entries on her list of Spotify liked songs. She created multiple playlists. The day before she'd left for Beaumont, she'd made two new playlists, one for the Clayton Holdings projects and one for Cordelia's wedding shower.

As Pink Floyd's "Learning to Fly," blasted through her computer speakers, Ione paused. The lyrics fit perfectly, not only for the project involving the eagles, but also her life. She'd once been a misfit, but as she'd aged she'd learned to embrace her quirks. That often meant she rubbed people the wrong way, no matter how hard she tried otherwise. It was simply who she was, and she'd accepted it.

Which was one reason why she couldn't wrap her head around Henry's change of heart. He'd sent her three texts in the course of an hour, which was three more than she'd ever received from him during the day when they'd been dating. Michael hadn't sent her any, not even to ask about her visit to the nest. Her emails had gone unanswered. She told herself he was a VP. He had multiple projects and things on his plate, including the fact that without Henry's sign-off, the nest relocation remained at a standstill. She didn't have anything new to tell him. If they hadn't had anything personal between them, Ione wouldn't think much of Michael's radio silence.

Instead, it bothered her. Her fingers itched to text him, but she refrained. She didn't want to appear too eager. Or, worse, needy. She'd made that mistake once before, in college, to embarrassing results. Appearing overzealous was the kiss of death, and she'd had enough of the Grim Reaper killing her relationships.

Not that this was a relationship. To squelch that line of thought, she turned her attention to the pollinator project. Creating new habitats for honeybees was something she could deal with. Although pollinators were any animals that moved pollen from flower to flower to accomplish fertilization, which meant she was also creating habitats for butterflies, moths, beetles and hummingbirds. To keep the environment pollinator friendly, Clayton Hotels had already established several wildlife corridors and had reduced its use of pesticides. Even the new golf course would use environmentally friendly techniques, like planting low-water grasses and native plants.

But Ione knew more could be done in Beaumont County. Clayton Holdings could sponsor joint educational projects at local schools. It could partner with local beekeepers, allowing them to maintain hives on specific parts of the Clayton Holdings acreage. Other projects involved planting more native plants on Clayton properties. In early spring, letting the unused fields flower instead of cutting them was another key way to help, along with establishing specific gardens that provided nectar and larval foods for the pollinators.

That Clayton Holdings was so committed made her job easy. There were so many things people could do on their own as well, and when she'd worked for the US Fish and Wildlife Service, she'd often tell people to not rake leaves in the fall so that animals had places to nest during the winter. If they were going to rake, they should leave piles of leaves in various places to help the animals. Many people knew to overseed their grass in the fall, but it was also important to scatter native seeds in fall gardens, as the seed's growth cycle needed the colder temperatures for a spring germination.

Ione saved her recommendations for Clayton's land-scapers. Letting out a long yawn, she leaned back. It was already a little after five. Arwen's ex had the kids for the weekend, so Arwen had taken their mom to her chemo treatment. Ione sent a text asking how things had gone. While waiting for an answer, she walked in circles on stiff legs to get the blood flowing. She clasped her hands behind her back and pressed her chest forward, loosening her back muscles. Her stomach growled, reminding her that she hadn't eaten. The granola bar after the hike didn't count. She had to stop forgetting about food. She examined the room-service menu. While everything sounded deli-cious, she couldn't decide. When her sister didn't reply, she sent her sister another text, this time just a question mark.

Sighing, Ione took a moment to answer Henry's last message: Still haven't heard from my sister. Not ignoring you. But don't have an answer yet.

Within seconds he'd liked the text and returned one of his own: With the guys. Will let you know when we're done.

Ione liked his message and then plopped herself on

the couch. Why was it that being in her hometown put her in such a funk? For someone who had a fantastic suite and didn't often go out, she had no idea why she was at such loose ends. Her typical Friday night, if she wasn't camping, was staying in and watching movies. Her hotel room had a big screen that was ideal for that.

But she didn't want to watch a movie. Going to Kaiser's was out. Ione didn't feel like sitting at the bar without her friends, and Will and Cordelia were heading into St. Louis for a concert. She startled as someone knocked on her door at the same time her phone pinged with a message: It's me

"Ione?" Michael called from the corridor.

She opened the door and Michael entered. He held up his hands in surrender "I know, I know. I should have called first. But I couldn't wait to see you." He turned to face her. "I have news. Good news. I've secured a wedding and reception venue for you."

"What?" The rush of excitement dissipated any apprehension caused by his popping by without asking. He'd come through for her. "You did it?"

"I did." A sexy swoop of hair fell over his right eye. "I hope you'll be pleased. Phyllis, our lead wedding coordinator at the Chateau, said that if Cordelia is willing to change her wedding time by two hours, then the Chateau can host both her wedding and reception in the French garden. Phyllis will install a gorgeous open-air tent and take care of everything, even contacting all the guests to let them know the time has changed. One miracle, as requested."

He'd done it. Delighted quivers traveled through Ione's veins and she resisted the urge to fling herself into his arms. "I saw pictures of the last reception the Chateau did like that. She'll love it. Oh, Michael. It's going to be perfect. She's going to be so happy!"

"And it comes with a bridal suite, which will be turned into a honeymoon suite during the reception."

The icing on the cake. Ione couldn't help herself. Her enthusiasm and delight won. She rushed forward, put both hands on either side of Michael's face and kissed him soundly. "Thank you!" She landed another kiss on his lips. "Thank you. Thank you!" She planted one last kiss before letting him go. Her lips still tingled.

"Ah, so this is what it takes to win your appreciation," Michael joked. He captured Ione's hands before she moved away. He flipped his wrist and glanced at the time. "Text her. Give her the good news, so that when Phyllis calls in the next fifteen minutes, Cordelia answers. Phyllis already has the contract from the Annex, so she knows the budget and Cordelia's preferences. She's going to accommodate everything."

"Everything?" The Chateau was the priciest, most exclusive venue in town.

"All of it," Michael confirmed.

Ione bit back happy tears. "This is unbelievable. I'm going to call her. She and Will are in the car." Ione stepped into her bedroom and closed the door. She dialed Cordelia.

"Hey, what's up?" Cordelia said.

"I have the best news." Several times she had to hold the phone out as Cordelia squealed in excitement.

"Ione, there's no way they can do all this on our budget," Cordelia finally said.

"Michael said it's covered. So when Phyllis calls, say yes," Ione insisted.

"Of course, I'm saying yes. You've just given me my dream wedding."

"Thanks, Ione!" Will called through the car's hands-free speaker.

Cordelia came back on. "Ione, you better not let this one go. Michael pulled those strings. He did this for you." Ione heard a beep. "That's her now. Gotta go!" With that, Cordelia clicked off.

When Ione returned to the living area, Michael was on the couch typing on his phone. He clicked the button that made the screen go black. She sat on the love seat perpendicular to him. "Is she excited?"

"She's ecstatic. She and Will looked at the Chateau, but they couldn't afford it. Did you do this for her?"

"Me?" Michael appeared to feign innocence. Then he turned serious. "You asked me to help. I helped. She'll be meeting with the planner tomorrow."

"Maybe there's a silver lining to all this. She wanted the Chateau. Thank you." Ione paused. "I'll hold up my end of the bargain and do some off-book hours."

Michael shook his head. "There's no need. I care for you, Ione, so that means by extension I care about the people you care about. I'm also going to look into what's going on with her rent. The Clayton family is here to help grow this town, not ruin it. I've got a note in my calendar to phone Jack. He and Sierra have been out of town."

"You're a good man," Ione said, meaning every word. How had she gotten so lucky as to meet him?

An eyebrow arched. "I hope you're not surprised by that."

She shook her head and rubbed a spot on her pants. "Not anymore. You're not your reputation." Her phone buzzed with a text from Henry. She ignored it.

"I'm glad you believe that. I means a lot." He shifted so he faced her more fully rather than in profile. "How was the hike to the nest?"

"Well, it was more a long hike through the conservation area all the way to the bluff. The nest isn't that far off the path, which is why it needs moving. Henry and I took the plans into the woods. We finished before the rain started. He said he'd get back with me later. Oh, I should show you the pics I took." Ione opened her phone to show him.

"Incredible," Michael said.

"It was. I feel bad moving the nest, but I know it's the right course of action." She glanced toward the window. Outside, the rain had lessened, but a light drizzle still fell. "It's been a rainy spring."

"Yeah. There are flood warnings in place. I'm glad you weren't caught in it." His worry touched her.

"My app alerted me. The water has nowhere to go. The Upper Midwest got six inches of rain last month, and that means the Missouri and the Mississippi are already near flood stage. The ground's already so wet, that if we get any more rain, it'll have nowhere to go. I studied the Great Flood of 1993 in college. It damaged Beaumont's riverfront."

"I read about that."

"The town founders, though, knew what they were doing when they built along Main Street and nothing lower. Sort of like New Orleans's French Quarter. Although that's sinking four centimeters a year."

Michael had tucked his lips together and was trying not to laugh.

She frowned. "What? Oh, I was babbling again, wasn't I?" She felt the heat rush to her cheekbones.

"I adore it," he said.

"What, that I'm a font of useless trivia?"

"No, that you're a font of awesome knowledge. That you're brainy and not afraid to show it. That makes you different. Better. Do you know how many women play dumb to get a man?"

"No, but I'd expect it's a few."

"More than there should be," he admitted. "In my case it's made worse because I have money. But not you. You are exactly who you are, and it's magnificent."

Her ego loved his compliments. "I don't think I've ever been thought of as magnificent before."

"Well, you should hear that you are more often." Ione's phone pinged again. "You should check that. Might be your mom."

She already knew it was Henry. "It's nothing I need to deal with. If it were my mom or Arwen, I'd look. It's odd I haven't heard from them today. I thought I'd be going over there. Maybe I should just go and drop in, the way you dropped in on me. But what if they don't want me to do that?"

"Why wouldn't they want you? You're family."

"Because I'm my mom's medical power of attorney. That means I know what the doctors do. She hates talking to me about her illness." And that was another reason Ione hadn't done any genetic testing. Her family had enough to worry about.

"It's okay not to be brave all the time, you know," Michael said.

"I can't help it. I don't want her to give up, to stop fighting because the treatment isn't working. Which means I'm always nagging, especially as I'm the one who makes decisions if she can't."

"That's a big responsibility."

"I'm not in town most of the time." On the off chance she'd missed something, Ione grabbed her phone. Henry was still with his coworkers at Miller's Grill, a Beaumont mainstay known for its delicious brisket. At the thought of food, her stomach rumbled. That's right, she'd been thinking of ordering food.

"You sound like you need to eat," Michael noted.

"I was trying to figure out dinner when you knocked," Ione admitted.

"Let's go get something," Michael suggested. "We'll stay close in case your sister gets back to you." But this time it was Michael's phone that pinged. He glanced at it and frowned.

"What's going on?" Ione asked.

"The rain's washed out a low water bridge on Chambers Road. The county is asking us if we'll open one of our private hotel roads so they can detour traffic. I need to make some calls. Do you want to meet me downstairs in about ten minutes?"

But ten minutes later, Ione was on her way to her sister's house. After texting both Michael and Henry about her change of plans, Ione drove to the outskirts of town and into one of the newer subdivisions, where

Arwen lived, and parked in the driveway to the right of her sister's SUV.

Arwen had opened the front door by the time Ione climbed onto the front porch. "Thank goodness you're here. I appreciate you canceling your plans," Arwen said, stepping out onto the front porch. Behind her, the front door remained open. "The kids have eaten and are in the family room. Mom's resting."

"Are you sure you don't want me to do the tour for you?" Ione offered.

"It's not a tour and I would say yes if you'd had time to prep. There's a convention in town and this is the historical background of Beaumont presentation."

"Okay, I'll hold down the fort."

"Thanks. I can't believe John canceled on me. The lawyer's gonna hear from me on Monday. Gotta go or I'll be late. Thanks for doing me a solid."

"Anytime." Ione accepted the air kiss that landed nowhere near her cheek. Ione watched her sister climb into the SUV, then stepped into the foyer and locked the front door. Arwen's house was typical of most two stories. To the right was a living room that Arwen used as an office, the desk piled high with papers. To the left was a formal dining room used only on major holidays. Straight back was the family room, where Ione found her niece and nephew playing video games. "Hey."

"Ione!" Paris, who was in sixth grade, hit Pause. At twelve and a dancer, Ione's niece was blooming in a way Ione hadn't at her age. "You came."

She made light of it. "Of course, I did. I couldn't let you hang here by yourselves."

"We don't need a babysitter." Roman set his controller aside. In ninth grade and a newly minted fifteen, he considered himself fully grown. "Grandma's here."

"Yes, but she's resting. While she does, I thought we'd go to LaBelle's and get some ice cream. It's still raining, but not as bad." And they didn't have to go anywhere near the flooding. "I haven't eaten. What did you have? Are you still hungry?"

Paris's nose wrinkled. "I am. It was leftovers. Mom didn't have time to cook anything."

"I wanted pizza." Roman clambered to his feet. Over the summer he'd shot up to almost five-ten, but the rest of him hadn't quite caught up.

"Tell you what, while they don't serve pizza, if you're still hungry you can get a burger and fries." That was met with enthusiasm, and after a short drive, they entered LaBelle's Diner, a restaurant operated as a side project of LaBelle Dairy. Unlike Miller's Grill, or the fancy eateries at the Grand and Chateau, LaBelle's was a 1950s throwback family diner, complete with a lunch counter that ran through half the space. Black vinyl booths lined the walls and chrome chairs with black cushions surrounded tables with black-and-white-checkerboard tops. Roman slid into the booth next to Paris, giving Ione an entire side to herself. Roman immediately studied the tri-fold laminated menu. "I'm having the burger, waffle fries and a Coke," he told their server.

Paris decided on cheese fries and a strawberry shake. Figuring a salad offset a chocolate shake, Ione ordered those. The food arrived quickly, and Paris chatted about her school's character council, something she'd joined. Roman's freshman baseball season had wrapped and he'd been moved up to JV. "If I do well enough I might be able to play varsity next year," he said. "Hey, I know some of those guys over there. Can I go say hi?"

"Sure." Ione wasn't a stickler for "may I," like her mom had been. She watched Roman cram into a booth with some friends before turning her attention back to Paris. Happy to have her aunt to herself, Paris began chatting about some of her friends and their crushes.

"Are you dating anyone?" Paris asked suddenly.

"Uh…" Caught off guard, Ione regrouped quickly. "My job makes it hard to date people."

"Because you're always going somewhere," Paris said, considering Ione's response. "But don't you want kids?"

It didn't matter what she wanted, or the longing she felt when she pictured how beautiful Michael's babies would be. Even a fraction of those genes would create adorable children. As Ione formulated an answer, Paris filled the silence.

"I wanted a sister for a while, but I'd settle for a cousin. I guess we'd be too far apart in age, but I could babysit. If you lived here and had kids, that is. I miss you."

The bittersweetness that was being home returned full force. "I miss you, too. I promise I'll visit as often as I can."

"You better," Paris insisted before filling her mouth with more cheese fries.

As Paris ate, Ione didn't miss the pang squeezing her heart. She loved her niece and nephew. She wanted a career and family. But Ione would never have that, and certainly not with Michael. It was an impossibility. Even if they could overcome the age gap, or the finances gap, or her nomadic lifestyle, the reality was that they weren't compatible long-term.

She wondered what Henry wanted. She didn't have overpowering feelings for him any longer, thanks to Michael. Still, Henry had been her world once. And she still needed a permit to remove the eagle's nest.

Paris waved a fry. "Aunt Ione, you're not listening to me."

"Sorry." Ione focused on what really mattered tonight—her family.

When they arrived back to the house forty-five minutes later, her mom was awake. Ione set the take-out bag on the bedside table. "I got you a grilled chicken sandwich from LaBelle's. Your favorite."

"I'm not that hungry." Her mom's hand trembled as she lifted the hospital-style cup and sipped from the straw.

Ione knew her mom's lack of appetite was a side effect of chemo, which was one reason she'd brought home the food. Anything to tempt her to eat. Even though her mom ate smaller portions five or six times a day, her weight loss had accelerated to the point of concern. She appeared shrunken against the white pillowcase, her cheekbones hollow and her skin pale. "Why don't you try a few bites?" Ione urged. "I had them add some cheddar cheese."

"It does smell good." Her mom set the cup on the rolling overbed table Ione had purchased. "Normally I can't smell anything."

"That's a good sign then." Ione busied herself with unwrapping and arranging the food. Using a knife, she cut the sandwich into quarters and handed her mother a section. "Here."

Her mom took a small bite, chewed and momentarily closed her eyes. When she opened them again, Ione thought she appeared a little brighter. "This is delicious. Thank you. I appreciate the thought."

"You know I'd do more if you let me."

"I'm fine," her mom said, waving off Ione's offer. "You girls worry too much. How's the job going?"

Recognizing the firm change of subject, Ione chose not to press and filled in her mother on the plan to relocate the eagle's nest.

"So you're dealing with Henry?" Her mom had eaten almost half the sandwich. She'd also had some of her protein shake. Ione took this as a positive.

"I am. He apologized. I don't know what to think about that. Henry never does anything without an agenda."

"Maybe he's changed," her mom said.

"Perhaps. But so I have I. The question is, what to do about it. Do I want to give him another chance? He humiliated me. Then again, you gave Dad another chance and fell in love and married."

"Your father was a good man. Henry never came to visit me once. I trust you'll figure it out." Her mom pointed at the food. "I'll eat more later. I need the restroom."

Her mother could use the bathroom by herself, so Ione rose and gathered the remains of the food. "I'm going to check on Paris and Roman, and then come back."

She found both kids in their respective bedrooms. Paris was writing while Roman was playing a video game on his handheld device. "How about a movie?" she asked. "Let's do a family night."

Which is where Arwen found them later when she returned home, watching something streaming on Netflix. Arwen set her backpack on the kitchen table as the credits started to roll. "How was it?"

"Better than I thought it would be," Paris said, earning a grunt of agreement from Roman.

"We've had a great time," their mom said, rising to her feet. She lifted a ceramic bowl that had once been filled with buttery popcorn. "It was a good film."

"Mom, I can carry that," Ione said.

"I wish I'd been here to see it," Arwen said.

"It was cute," Ione said, tracking her mom's progress. She moved slowly but steadily. However, when she entered the kitchen, the bowl slipped from her fingers and landed on the floor, the pieces shattering. Ione winced.

Everyone froze for a split second as the sound reverberated. Then they began moving. "Do not touch those pieces," Arwen told her mother, who was stooping low.

"I'll grab the broom," Paris said, already headed around the mess toward the laundry room.

"Hey, Grandma, how about I help you?" Roman had taken her arm and was guiding her toward the stairs. "Let's get you into the bathroom so you can wash your hands."

Ione turned the TV off. Arwen had found the trash can and was dropping the larger pieces of the bowl into it. Paris was sweeping shards and popcorn kernels into the dustpan. Her mother and Roman had disappeared out of sight. "What can I do?" she asked. Other than insisting she take the bowl, which, while embarrassing to her mother, would have avoided all this.

"There's a vacuum cleaner and Swiffer in the laundry room. Once Paris sweeps, I'll run the vacuum, then mop the floor. If you could grab those for me and then check on Mom, that would be great."

"I can do that." Ione found the items and came back. "How often does this happen?"

Arwen waited until Paris went upstairs. "She's getting weaker. We need the money for the new treatment. With the divorce, I don't have enough equity in the house to take out a second, but I can do an unsecured loan—"

"No." Ione's interruption came out sharper than she intended. "You take care of her and I'll find the money. You've got kids and college payments in a few years. I'll figure this out. I don't have people depending on me like you do. And I feel bad about this. I worried she'd drop it but didn't want to strip away even more of her pride."

"It doesn't matter. Don't worry about it. You don't live here. We don't expect you to live here. Someone has to save the world, Ione. That's you. We'll deal with Mom."

That was her sister, always putting others before herself and her needs. "But I need to help save my family, too."

Arwen grimaced. "And you do, by paying for things. Don't think I don't know what you already do. You've given up things to work and support Mom. Leave me some pride, okay?"

"It's not my intention to make you feel any less worthy." Shocked, Ione tried to backtrack and salvage the situation. "And is it really giving up things when no one wants to marry me? Like I have to face the fact that maybe marriage isn't in my future. And I don't know if I carry the genetic markers."

"I don't," Arwen said.

That surprised Ione. "Oh. I didn't realize…"

"That I got tested? Of course, I did. I have two children who depend on me. When Mom got sick again, I asked my doctor. I'm good, Ione. Get tested. Stop being a martyr. Let the guilt go. It's like worry. It does no good to do either. Same for fear. All guilt, worry and fear do is suck energy best used elsewhere. Stop thinking you need to carry the world on your shoulders. You don't. The rest of us are capable of doing some heavy lifting. You don't have to do it alone."

"You're right. But it's hard."

Arwen dumped a dustpan worth of ceramic shards into the trash can. "Life is hard. Look at me. My marriage is a failure. My tour business is stagnant. But I choose to focus on hope and joy. Things are already negative. I don't need to compound it by looking at the glass half-empty."

Ione impulsively gave Arwen a hug. "You're amazing."

Arwen attempted a smile and leaned back. "I don't know about that. But I've learned to control the things I can control. That's the best I can do."

Ione decided to take that to heart as she let Arwen go. "I'll go check on Mom," Ione offered.

"Don't bother." Roman's feet pounded down the stairs. "She washed up and climbed into bed. Told me to shut the door on my way out and not to let either of you disturb her."

"She's being stubborn again," Arwen said. "But it means she's fighting, at least."

"I'll take it," Ione said.

Roman grabbed the vacuum and the loud noise ended the conversation. Soon, the kitchen had been put to rights. A glance at Ione's watch told her it was almost eleven. "It's late. I'll check in with you in the morning."

"Are you sure you don't want to stay overnight? I make pancakes on Saturday mornings."

The offer tempted her but Ione had work to do. "Next time. It's not that far to the hotel and I'm wide-awake. Tomorrow I need to deal with Cordelia's bridal shower prep. You'll be there Sunday afternoon, right?"

"Mom and I wouldn't miss it. Roman and Paris are fine staying home alone if John doesn't take them somewhere."

"Doubtful my dad's getting us." Roman toed the clean floor with the tip of his tennis shoe, and then, as if realizing his mom was about to say something about his attitude, he quickly added, "Good night, Aunt Ione. See you soon," then gave her a hug and ran back upstairs.

"Text me when you're back," Arwen said. That was her sister, always ensuring everyone was safe.

"I will." Ione gathered her things and dashed through the rain. The wipers swished at top speed, allowing Ione to see the road closure set up on the outskirts of town. Yellow lights flashed on top of traffic barricades, so Ione followed a detour that wound and twisted its way through the hills before connecting with Winery Road. She pulled under the hotel portico and texted her sister: Here. Detour on River Road added ten minutes. Be prepared for that Sunday.

Her sister liked the message and Ione entered the hotel and began to cross the lobby. As she approached the elevators, one of the private elevators opened and Michael stepped out. He wore a dark blue business suit and loosened red tie. He appeared slightly harried. "Hey. What are you doing here?"

"Oh, after you went to your sister's, I caved to Eva's sisterly pressure and attended the chamber-of-commerce meeting with her. Since we hosted it here, I commandeered a penthouse for the night since I didn't want to drive in this weather. One of the low-water bridges is impassible, but the Missouri is also rising faster than expected. The person who's in charge of our crisis team is on paternity leave, and the manager who he'd brief is on vacation, and since I'm here, I'll handle things."

"I drove the detour on my way back," Ione told him, still considering the fact he would have skipped a chamber meeting to see her instead.

"Any other issues?" He peered at her with concern.

"No. I'm hoping we get a break in the rain for Cordelia's bridal shower Sunday. Although we'll be inside at Elephant Rock, so it should be fine. Tomorrow I'm prepping for that in between working on the next meeting with the feds."

"Good. So did you have a good visit with family? How's your mom?"

Michael's concern touched her, and she blinked rapid-fire to contain the tears. "My mother's not doing well. It was hard. And my sister…" She stepped out of the way of people needing the elevator.

"Do you want to talk about it? The bar's open until one, or…" He tilted his head toward the express elevator. "Come on." The doors slid open and he pressed his key to send the car upward. "I know how you like privacy." He unlocked a suite larger than most one-bedroom apartments. She sat on the couch and he brought her a glass of water. "What's going on?" he asked.

Ione filled him in on her mom's condition and current state. "That's why this next bonus is so important. Once I get it, I can pay for the experimental treatment."

"That's a lot of pressure."

She nodded, appreciating that he didn't offer her money, which she wouldn't have taken.

"Parents matter, and it's hard when they're sick. Mine may give me tons of grief, but if something happened to them, I'd move heaven and earth to help them."

He sipped from his own glass, drawing her attention to the line of his throat. "There's a reason my siblings and I want my dad to retire, or at least step back. He had a health scare a few years back, and while it turned out to be nothing major, it was a wake-up call for all of us. Parents are supposed to live forever, you know?"

"I do. And that's rough. Losing my dad still hurts. Not as much as it once did, but there are times when I want to talk to him and…"

"I'm sorry."

"My family had a lot of support. That helped."

"We had to keep it quiet. Even though we're not a public company, we do have a lot of stakeholders. Instability in leadership can spark panic, which is why there are certain things the press doesn't need to know. Speaking of things you need to know, after a meeting tomorrow morning, I'm flying to Portland. There's a charity event that I have to attend and then meetings Monday morning. I should be back Tuesday morning. Shall we plan to do lunch Tuesday afternoon? That way you can fill me in on everything. We can eat in one of the conference rooms. I'll have food brought in."

"Sure." She entered the information in her phone's calendar. "It's a date." Her word choice made Michael groan. Her eyebrows knitted together. "What? Why are you staring at me like that?"

"I want to take you on a real date."

"Do we need one?" They'd been as close as two humans could be.

Michael shifted to sit by her, and her hands tingled when he took them in his. "Of course, we do. You're smart, kind, beautiful and sexy. I like you. I enjoy talking to you. I like kissing you. Besides chemistry, there's something more here that I want to explore. I want a real date, Ione. I don't want to be kept in the shadows."

"Oh." The thought boggled.

"We can wait until after your projects are done. But I want to take you out. I don't know who did a number on your head, but I'd like to give him a piece of my mind."

Those words sobered the giddiness, so Ione said nothing. That wouldn't be a good idea, especially with Henry needing to sign off on Michael's permits.

Michael seemed to interpret her silence for disbelief. "I'm not slumming with you, Ione."

She still didn't understand. He could have any woman he wanted and she wasn't part of his world. "I'm the exact opposite of you."

"Then we're a perfect case of opposites attracting. Together, we make something pretty good. Which is why I want a real date. I don't need a bed warmer. I want a companion. Someone to love. A family."

The latter of which, she couldn't give anyone. Not

until she knew. And Michael deserved more than an older woman whose career and family came first. "Your life is here. Mine is across the globe, wherever my company sends me. You know why I have to go." She pulled her hands from his. If she kept touching him, she'd cave. "It's not fair to you."

"That's not fair to us. Don't I get to also be the judge of that?"

"There is no us. I mean, I enjoyed having sex with you. I wouldn't mind more. But…"

"Priorities," Michael said, finishing for her. He shifted and put space between them. Shoved his hands between his knees.

"That's a good description for it. Like, I could kiss you now. I want to." She wanted nothing more. Well, maybe world peace and a stop to climate change. But as for desires, how easily it would be to take his hand again and lead him through the open bedroom door on the other side of the suite.

"I do want you," she told him. "But if we start kissing, I don't know if I could stop. And that wouldn't be fair to either of us. You want something more and I can't give you what you want. Not beyond the physical. And you're trying to turn over your new leaf. You're worth more than taking what you can get. Perhaps we need to leave what happened between us in the past. As much as we may not want to. As much as our biological natures want otherwise."

"It's more than biology."

"Maybe." Like in that Pixar movie, with the characters portraying emotions, Ione could almost hear her body's desire shouting inside her head that she was making a huge mistake in turning him down. But her logical brain overruled her longing with a lecture on priorities.

"I understand."

She rose. "I should go. Thank you for not pressuring me."

Michael stood but didn't move closer. "I don't know who he was, but he's not me. I would never do that."

Which made him different from any other man she'd ever disappointed. Her head began to throb, as if the emotions bouncing around inside had gotten into a knock-down, drag-out fight. "Thank you." She moved and gave him a quick kiss on his cheek. "I'll see you later."

One foot in front of the other, Ione told herself as she headed toward the door. Don't look back. Head high, but not haughty. Don't turn around. If she did, she'd race back to his arms and never leave.

The door opened with an ominous click and made another as she closed it behind her. She moved automatically into the elevator, allowing herself to slump against the smooth wall once she'd pressed the button for her floor. She might be making one of the hugest mistakes of her life. And that already included starting a relationship with Henry.

Add this to the list.

Chapter Nine

"You look like you sucked on a lemon," Eva observed Saturday evening. She took another shrimp skewer from the roving server, slid the morsel into her mouth and placed the toothpick in the silver container on the server's tray.

Michael hadn't eaten any of the perfectly crafted appetizers passing by. He hadn't even sipped the two fingers of bourbon he held in his right hand. He was standing in a beautiful ornate room, a showcase really, reflecting the grandeur of what was the first Clayton Hotel, but he wanted to be anywhere else, and counted down the minutes until he could leave.

"Snap out of it," Eva told him as she adjusted his cuff link. "You need to smile and make pleasant conversation."

"That's your job."

Eva tugged his sleeve in exasperation. "It's Margot Van Horn's birthday. And since we now own her hotels, act happy and be nice. If she asks, we gave her a Tiffany collar for her favorite cat."

"As long as she's not thrusting her granddaughter at me, I'll be on my best behavior."

"I don't think you're Sophie's type, so you can stop worrying. There's no one in attendance that will give you an ounce of worry…" Eva stopped. "Crud. I jinxed it."

"What?" Michael turned to see whom she'd seen. "Oh, great. Just what I needed."

His ex, Rachel, was heading in their direction. She looked the same as when he'd seen her last—minus the snarling expression. Her face was perfectly made up and her designer dress was the latest style.

"Smile," Eva hissed and Michael managed to plaster on the appropriate pleasant yet disinterested expression as Rachel approached.

"Michael," Rachel said, leaning to give him a kiss on the cheek. Aware that the roving photographers snapped the interaction, Michael managed not to cough as her expensive yet cloying perfume filled his nostrils. He also held still as her fingertips wiped her red lipstick from his skin.

"Rachel. Nice to see you. How are you?" He spoke with warm familiarity of someone greeting an old friend they hadn't seen in a long while. That earned him a pleased nod from Eva before someone diverted his sister's attention.

Her departure meant Rachel was free to ease into Michael's space. "Thank you for asking. I'm well. Heading up the charity gala for the child-services foundation. I can count on you to make your normal auction donation, can't I?"

He managed not to frown. Had she just batted her eyelashes at him?

"Of course." To raise money for the organization, each year Clayton Holdings donated a three-night stay in the penthouse of any of its Clayton Hotels resorts, including all global hotels. "Our charitable-giving department chair hasn't changed. Last year's coordinator should have her contact information. You can reach out on Monday."

"That's so generous of you. I will." Rachel's lips formed a playful pout, the one that had once captured his attention. What had he seen in her? As he studied Rachel's perfectly low-cut yet respectable designer gown, Michael didn't know. Perhaps he'd been blinded by his own immaturity and his place in the young Portland society crowd. While the playboy label might have described him at one time, now, he was an executive running a global hotel chain. He'd matured. Learned what mattered. And he'd found the one woman he couldn't have, one whose commitment to her job, family and environment made her more real than the woman in front of him. Ione didn't play at being charitable. She got into the trenches to find real solutions. Rachel was his past. Ione, Michael thought determinedly, was his future. He just had to convince her to give them a chance.

Rachel didn't notice his silence, or if she did, she ignored it. "How have you been? We've missed you in Portland."

Michael hadn't missed Portland much, if at all. He was like one of Ione's pollinator butterflies, having left his old form behind. "I like Beaumont far more than I ever thought I would. And my family is there."

"I heard about Liam's wedding. We were all abuzz here. And he has twins."

"Yes. Two girls. My nieces are adorable." Michael wished Eva would return to rescue him, but she'd disappeared. And he didn't see anyone close enough that he could say "excuse me, I need to see them" without appearing rude. That was the last thing he needed—he'd be vilified in social media as being cruel if he walked away abruptly, as he longed to do.

Rachel gave a slight sigh and pushed forward. "I want to apologize for what happened last fall. Brittany and I had a huge falling-out over it once I calmed down. She never should have pretended to be me and come on to you like she did. She was just jealous of me."

"It doesn't matter." Michael ignored her attempt to revise history and craned his head, trying to locate Eva. He'd give her one minute and then rudeness be damned.

The event photographer approached holding a DSLR camera, and he waved the two of them together. Rachel slid an arm around Michael's back and placed the other on his arm. The man took the picture and then left.

"But it does matter," Rachel said, picking up the thread, but not her hand from Michael's arm. "We had a good thing going, and I let it go. I was wrong. I've wanted to tell you that in person. I've missed you. I miss what we had."

He wasn't waiting another minute to extricate himself. "It was for the best, as I was moving to Beaumont. I wish you well, Rachel, truly, but I've moved on. I hope we can be friends."

Perhaps he was jaded, but as he freed himself from her grasp, he didn't think she'd be too crushed. She wanted him because he was Michael Clayton, VP. Not because of any other reason. They'd been a great power couple, not much more. Eva was right. Time and distance in Beaumont had given Michael much-needed perspective.

Speaking of Eva, he finally spotted her across the room with Margot Van Horn. He gave Rachel a curt nod. "Be sure you contact our giving coordinator on Monday. Just remember that she's in Beaumont now, and two hours ahead. Good seeing you, Rachel. Excuse me."

With that, Michael left her standing there and wove his way over to his sister and Margot. Margot gave him a huge smile. "Ah, here's my favorite VP."

"Here's my favorite retiree and birthday girl." Like a dutiful, adopted grandson, Michael kissed her elderly cheek. Out of Rachel's orbit, he began to relax. "You're what, seventy-five again?"

"For the last several years," Margot said, accepting the flattery. "When I hit eighty maybe I'll claim it."

Michael dialed up the attention. He'd gotten to know Margot well once they'd finalized the acquisition of her hotels. "Never. Have you slowed down yet? I don't think so."

Margot's laugh was genuine. "And minus letting you steal my hotels, I don't plan on it. I have way too much to do."

Which probably meant donating more money to cat charities, something she'd asked for in lieu of birthday gifts as her four-thousand-square-foot mansion housed dozens of rescue animals. Margot might stand before him in designer blue sequins with her white hair in a chignon, but she was a true eccentric with a heart of gold.

She'd had his brother Edmund go undercover on a TV show her grandson had been producing in order to win the right to buy her hotels. Edmund had lost, but he'd met Lana. In the end, he'd won both the hotels and the girl. Michael had learned a lot from Margot, whose business acumen fit that adage that she'd forgotten more than he would ever know. "I see you left your admirer."

Rachel was already deep in conversation with Thaddeus Raymond IV. "She and I were over last fall."

"Good. She never did suit you, but she might Thaddeus. You're better off without her. Eva tells me you've settled down." Margot chuckled at his dour expression. "Now, now, I wanted to hear it from someone other than you. Besides, I seem to have a good influence on getting you Clayton boys to settle down."

"True," Michael agreed. "If Edmund hadn't met Lana, then Liam and I never would have gone to Beaumont."

Margot chuckled. "Who knew Edmund would give everything up for love. But you boys constantly surprise me. It's been fun watching you grow up."

Margot was one of Michael's grandmother's best friends, so she'd known him since birth. "Well, I'm trying," he told her, noting Eva had wandered off again. "I've met someone, but she's not impressed by me and won't let me take her out on a date."

"She sounds like a smart woman."

"Why does everyone keep saying that?"

The twinkle in Margot's eye told Michael she was teasing him.

"But she does have a PhD. She's a wildlife biologist. She'd rather be camping than at an event like this."

"She might surprise you. If you truly care for her, which I can tell from your eager puppy-dog expression that you do, don't give up. Prove to her your worth. Give without expecting anything in return. What can you do to make her life easier? Show her that you'll be there through good times and bad. But don't just be a check-book or status symbol, which is what Rachel wanted. Be more."

"How?" Michael asked, genuinely wanting to know.

"You'll have to figure that out on your own. But if you do win her over, I expect you to bring her to me so I can meet her. You're my favorite, you know. Just don't tell your brothers."

"You probably say that to them when you're alone."

Margot shook her head. "Actually, I don't." She turned as a man approached. "Ah, Lachlan, here you are. Michael, you remember my grandson, right?"

The man who'd produced Edmund's undercover show joined them, and they chatted for a moment more before Michael made his way to the bar. He'd set aside his full glass of bourbon a while ago, and he wanted some water. Then he'd go upstairs and get some sleep. Missouri was two hours ahead, so it was almost 1:00 a.m. in Beaumont.

He allowed himself a smile. Not only was he grow-ing up, but he was also turning into an old man out past his bedtime. He grabbed the plastic cup the bartender passed over and left the ballroom. Margot's words had made sense. It was time to perform some more Clayton miracles to win the girl of his dreams.

Besides the near constant rain, Cordelia's wedding shower was an epic success. The staff at Elephant Rock winery had gone above and beyond in making the day special, including upgrading the cake from a sheet to three tiers decorated with *viola pedata*, or birdfoot violets, made out of sugar. The real flowers, found naturally in Missouri, showcased Cordelia's wedding colors of light yellow and pale purple.

"Ione, you need to keep him," Cordelia said as they watched Will pack the car with bridal shower gifts. He'd arrived at the end of the shower to drive Cordelia home. "You know Michael did this for me because of you."

"I'm sure he had nothing to do with it." Ione ignored her, despite her suspicion Cordelia was right. "He's in Portland. And he's not in charge of the wineries. That's Liam." Whom Ione had learned was back in town. He'd be joining the pollinator project meetings in a few days.

"You keep telling yourself that," Cordelia said. "I had my doubts about Michael, but he's come through. And if my wedding is as lovely as the coordinator promised it was going to be, Ione, that will be a dream come true. You won't believe all the things she told me the Chateau is going to do for me."

"I'm sure they'll do the same for other brides who had their weddings scheduled at the Annex."

Cordelia sighed. "You can be so stubborn sometimes. He clearly likes you. Go on a date with him. What can it hurt?"

"My career? Henry's pride?" Ione had told Cordelia about her and Michael's conversation. "I may not want my ex, but you know how petty Henry can be at times. I don't want to risk any of the permitting. I need him to sign off on things."

"But you shouldn't have to sell your soul or give up something that might be awesome just to make Henry happy. You deserve happiness, too."

Will approached. "All the gifts are loaded."

Cordelia gave Ione a hug. "Remember what I said. At least think about it. He's the complete package."

"Who's the complete package?" Will asked.

"I'll tell you in the car," Cordelia said, kissing his cheek before taking his hand. Ione watched them walk away. Will and Cordelia had a love that simply radiated. While that wasn't scientific, it was the best description. And though she was happy for her friend, she couldn't help but feel a small twinge of longing that she would someday have the same type of love.

Ione's mom approached. "Fabulous shower. Even if it rained. You did well." Ione's mom looked brighter today, as if she'd rested well last night. "It's good to see Cordelia so happy."

"Yeah. I'm glad she enjoyed this."

"I overhead a little of your conversation. Perhaps you should do as she suggests. You deserve to be happy, too."

"Mom," Ione protested as Arwen joined them. She did not want to discuss this now. "Let's get everyone home."

Since they'd taken two cars, Ione drove back to the hotel on her own. She found Henry waiting in the lobby. "Here you are," he said. "I was about to text you."

Juggling the small gift bag filled with party favors, Ione frowned. "Did we have an appointment?"

"No, but I was over here for a late lunch with Beverly Jean. She'd heard the food was fabulous and wanted to try it."

The Grand's food was expensive and the words were out before she could call them back. "The government only gives you a certain per diem."

Henry's benevolent expression told Ione he found her concern silly.

"Yes, I know that. As does she. We paid for part of our lunches ourselves. Really, Ione, you should give me more credit. We had *linner*, as Beverly Jean called it. A combination of lunch and dinner. We discussed the nest and my thoughts."

They'd met on a Sunday. "You haven't even shared those with me yet," Ione said, slightly put out.

"Because you've been busy." Henry soothed. "You're the one who's canceled. I've wanted to see you time and time again. You're overreacting."

"Sorry." The word was automatic, as something about Henry's attitude rubbed her the wrong way and she wanted to defuse the situation. "Shall we go into the bar and discuss your thoughts now? I have a different expense account than you do."

"If that's your way of asking me if I'd have a drink with you, then I'm happy to accept since you're free now."

She'd intended to go to the hotel gym to run off the extra slice of cake and two glasses of nonalcoholic punch she'd had at the bridal shower, while everyone else had enjoyed raspberry-flavored bubbly. "Now is perfect." Better to get this over with.

"Excellent. I'm so glad we can finally catch up." Henry placed his hand lightly on her back and guided her toward the Grand's bar. Ione liked the vibe. The tables and barstools were dark stained wood, the chairs overstuffed and the ambience cozy and quaint with the type of subdued lighting that made everyone look great. He chose a quiet booth in the far corner. "I'm glad we finally connected. How's your mother?"

"She seemed better today."

"That's great news. You've been worried about her. Which makes me concerned about you. How are you holding up?"

"Fine."

His smile was the same tolerant one used on a young child. "Of course, you are. Do you know how many times you used that exact word when we were dating?"

She bristled. How dare he placate her. "I am fine. I solve problems. I am handling things. What did you and Beverly Jean discuss? Are you going to issue Clayton Hotels the permits they need?"

"Always straight to business." Henry's tiny head-shake seemed more indulgent than intolerant. "We'll get to that."

A server took their order. Ione chose her usual—one glass of red wine and one glass of water. Keeping with tradition, Henry ordered draft beer. "Did you eat?"

"We had a fried-chicken buffet at the winery. Cordelia's bridal shower was today." She pointed to the gift bag.

"I'm sure it was lovely. You always saw her when you came back to Beaumont. You must like being closer to home than when you were in Alaska."

"I'm not close enough," Ione said. "Although Atlanta is a far shorter plane ride."

"Would Minneapolis be closer? It didn't take me long to fly to Beaumont."

"Perhaps, but why would I go there?" She wished he'd get to the point, but knew better than to trigger him by saying that.

He fingered the black paper cocktail napkin. "To see me, maybe? I've missed you."

"You said I was boring." She couldn't help herself.

He tore off a corner and let the little black triangle sit in the middle of the table. "And I've apologized for being hurtful. I was wrong. I've missed you. I want to settle down."

"With me?" Once she would have been ecstatic about his declaration. It had been her hope and dream.

He picked another corner loose. "Why not? We made a good team."

They had. But they hadn't made a good couple outside of work. "We mixed business with pleasure. We were unhappy."

"We had one fight. I can make you happy. You just need to forgive me."

She shook her head. "What would make me happy is having the permits to remove the eagles' nest. You know they'll come back to the area during the next migration."

"Beverly Jean said the same thing. Which is why I'm going to recommend that we allow the nest to be removed and given to the Missouri Department of Conservation. With some feathers for DNA, of course. I'll sign off on that, too."

"Henry, I…" Finally. She nodded. "Thank you. This makes me happy." Not that she'd tell Michael until all was signed, sealed and delivered. She'd been down that road before.

"I'm glad I can make you happy. In the end, this was also the practical choice. It's in everyone's best interests, including the town, and the higher-ups agree. And you are right. The eagles will return unless something happens to them when they fly north."

"Nothing will happen to them." Ione predicted. "They'll be fine."

"Protecting nature is why I went into this job. I'm not letting some bad actors harm our national treasures. Not on my watch."

Ione sighed her relief. "The Claytons aren't bad actors. Trust me, I'm as passionate as you about making a difference. I hate that some people can be so cruel and inhumane." She lifted her water, choosing not to touch her wine yet.

Henry drank his beer. "I'm glad you didn't lose your convictions when you went into the private sector. I worried about that."

"Never. My company has ethics or I wouldn't work there."

"I worked with one recently that didn't. Needless to say, they didn't like it when I didn't give them what they wanted." After Henry began to explain, they fell into the same easy conversational pattern as they'd had when they'd worked together. They'd always had similar philosophies and approaches to problem solving. Henry's mind challenged hers, which was one of things that had first attracted her to him. It didn't hurt that he was good-looking.

Relaxing, Ione drank her wine slowly, making it last as the evening waned into the dinner hour and she and Henry split an appetizer. She was laughing at something he said when a voice she knew well said, "Don't you two look cozy."

"Michael!" Ione sobered immediately, not that she was tipsy. "You're back early. I thought you were staying in Portland."

"I moved things around. Mind if I join you?" His face inscrutable, Michael slid in next to her and Ione scooted over to give him space. Michael shot out his hand across the table. "Henry. Good to see you again."

Henry shook Michael's hand. "Same. You were out of town?"

"A brief trip back to Portland. Former home of Clayton Holdings. We're now one hundred percent in Beaumont. I had a birthday party to attend. I rescheduled tomorrow's meetings. While our corporate office is not in a floodplain, there's concern the town's going to need to sandbag, as well as some of the outlying areas. To make sure everyone has the help they need, we gave everyone the day off. The levees should hold. They were rebuilt and reinforced after the Great Flood of 1993."

"I didn't realize you were so keyed into the status of river water," Henry said.

Michael didn't blink. "I've got reports coming at me constantly. As does my brother Liam. Excess rain can impact grape growth. If the soil is too waterlogged, the roots suffocate and the vines rot. That impacts the harvest."

"I didn't know that," Ione said.

"Picked up a few things from my brother. Liam can't have all the fun." Michael's grin failed to touch his gorgeous gray eyes and Ione sensed something was off.

"Speaking of fun, this has been great to catch up, but I'm sure you have places to be," Henry told Michael in a subtle hint that even Ione could understand. She frowned at her ex.

"You should tell him your decision about the eagles,"

Ione inserted quickly, trying to defuse the situation. "Before he goes. You know, about the permits."

Henry gave a dramatic show of waving his beer, as if trying to demonstrate the magnitude of his decision. "As long as the paperwork is in order, I don't see a problem with your request to remove the nest. We'll approve it as long as the paperwork is filled out correctly and to my satisfaction."

"Then I should start on that right away." Ione shifted, facing Michael. "It's been a lovely evening, but I should get to work."

The server came over. "Put their bill on my tab," Michael instructed.

"That's so generous of you," Ione said. She needed Michael to move and let her out. When his leg accidentally pressed hers, even an unintentional touch sent desire racing through her.

"Yeah, thanks," Henry said, "but I'll pay my way as to not have a conflict of interest." He tossed some bills on the table.

"Suit yourself." As if recognizing Ione's need to leave, Michael slid out of the booth and held out his hand to assist her. For the short duration her hand was in his, her fingers tingled with warmth, desire and promise. When Henry rose, the three of them stood at the table, the moment awkward. As the two men sized each other up, Ione stepped out of the way. They reminded her of two stags about to fight, which made little sense. Never before had she been the subject of such obvious male posturing and she hated it. First, there was Henry, who so clearly wanted to keep the evening going, and Michael, who so blatantly was blocking Henry's wishes.

Ione coughed to get their attention. The last thing she needed was for Henry to change his mind about the removal of the nest.

"Gentlemen, this has been wonderful, but I'm headed to my room. Henry, it was great catching up. Michael, I'll see you in the office tomorrow."

Before either could reply, she turned on her heel, moving as casually as she could toward the exit. She refused to look back, lest she give her conflicting feelings away.

The fact was, she'd choose Michael every time, not that her decision was like shopping for apples at the supermarket. In this case, while she longed for things to proceed with Michael, she couldn't risk her heart. Eventually men found her lacking. Henry had and would again. Michael was still in the thrill of the chase. She was sensible enough that she knew they'd both move on. Best to call it quits on her terms.

As Michael watched Ione walk away, that innate sense of alpha male let him know Henry was doing the same. "Thank you for the permits," Michael told him. "We can chat details while I walk you out. I appreciate you filling Ione in on your decision and look forward to partnering with you."

As the men moved toward the exit, he received a grunt in acknowledgement before Henry said, "How long is Ione's contract with Clayton Holdings?"

Michael schooled his face and resisted asking why Henry wanted to know. "Our contract with Good-4 Environmental is open-ended. Liam wants pollinator habitats at our wineries and resorts, so Ione is overseeing that project as well as the eagles."

"Did you request Ione?"

Michael found the question odd, and he wanted to pry. "We did not request a specific consultant. Good-4 Environmental sent her as she'd finished a project in West Virginia and was available. I'm sure the prospect of having some time in her hometown appealed to her, and we're grateful she knows the area. She's been a huge asset already."

"Hmm," Henry mumbled noncommittally.

"I understand you used to work together." Michael's curiosity won out.

"We did more than work together. We dated. I made a mistake in breaking things off a year ago."

Michael had a great deal of experience with being shocked. After all, he'd been named a VP out of the blue. He excelled at rolling with the punches and coming out on the other side without missing a beat. He'd been through scandal after scandal and held his held high. That adage Never Let Them See You Sweat fit him to a *T*. But as he snapped shut his mouth, he realized he'd ceded the upper hand. This revelation had thrown him for the proverbial loop.

"I can see I've surprised you," Henry said.

That was an understatement. This was the guy that had treated Ione like crap? The reason she'd wanted one night last October to wipe the slate clean? It was all Michael could do to keep himself calm. He hated being blindsided. He also hated how Henry had hurt Ione.

Managing to recover his composure, Michael banished the immediate urge to give Henry a piece of his mind and instead allowed a nonchalant shrug that would have made his sister proud. Eva always managed to be unflappable in a crisis.

"Ione's personal life is her own," Michael said, his tone level with just the right touch of nonissue boredom. "She's here to do a job, and we're pleased with her work."

Taking Michael's words at face value, Henry nodded. "That's good to hear. She told me tonight how much she's enjoying working as a consultant. I'm happy she's found something she loves doing. It became too much, us dating and working together."

Michael wasn't sure if he agreed with that assessment, especially given that Edmund and Lana worked together. But Henry was clearly ready to share. "That's where we went wrong. Working relationships can develop too much conflict. Gonna try to fix that now that we're in the same field but in different capacities. She's special, you know."

Michael did know. But he said nothing. Ione had wanted to keep her and Michael's relationship—could he even call it that?—a secret, and now Michael fully understood why. He didn't like it one bit.

"A man gets to a certain age and it's time to settle down, especially at this point in my career," Henry said. He and Michael were under the portico waiting for the valet.

"And you think Ione's it?"

"Why not? We're compatible in many ways and we're both passionate about the environment. She can work from home when she has children…"

Michael frowned at the man but somehow hid his total disgust. That didn't sound like love. It sounded more like a matter of social convenience, but then maybe Henry was as analytical and practical as Ione was blunt and forthright. Unwilling to hear any more of the future Henry was planning with the woman Michael was falling for, Michael interrupted Henry's spiel. "Listen, this is delving into personal territory, and until we have signed permits, I'm not sure we should be discussing your intentions toward her. She's my family's consultant under contract with us. That can be seen as a conflict of interest."

"I get it. I just wanted you to know where I stood, and that my intentions are honorable."

"I never doubted that they were," Michael said, not believing him. He also understood that Henry was clearly marking his territory. "But I don't want anything to go wrong between you two before our deal is done. You can understand that concern."

"We'll finish the permits tomorrow," Henry promised. "That way we can all move on."

"Fantastic. Looking forward to it," Michael said, using an efficient business-like enthusiasm he didn't feel. He'd planned on coming to the hotel tonight and sweeping Ione off her feet. Instead, he'd run into her ex—the ex who'd made her leave Alaska—and discovered the man planned on winning her back. What a mess. Michael should cut and run. Leave Ione to her own devices. If any of this got out, the PR would be a nightmare. The influencers and pundits would live it up. Not only was there a secret love triangle, but the permitting could also be considered suspect, as Henry's motivations could be seen as an attempt to win back his ex, who was consulting for Clayton. Favoritism was a dirty word, and while Eva was a magician when it came to handling bad press, even she would have her back against the wall with this situation.

Once again, it all came down to the fact that Michael should have kept his pants zipped. But something about Ione drove him to madness. He wanted her. He also wanted his permits, so his father got off his case.

Michael shook Henry's hand and watched as the man drove off in his government-issued vehicle. He waited until the taillights disappeared before asking the valet to retrieve his car. While he wanted to talk to Ione, she was working on his project. And he wanted some time and distance first. He used the hands-free settings to make a call. Despite being in Portland, Eva answered on the first ring. "Hey, what's up? Don't tell me you did something stupid."

"It's still the same old stupid," Michael said. "Me."

"You have got to be kidding me," Eva said once he'd filled her in. The car's speakers emphasized her sympathy and outrage on his behalf.

"I wish I was," Michael said. "How do I get myself in these messes?"

"Look, go home. Rest. We'll talk more tomorrow once I get there. Let's get these permits secured. I'm sure that's why she didn't tell you. She wasn't wanting to jeopardize anything."

"I hope that's all." Michael ended the call and followed the signs marking the detour. He parked his car behind the art gallery. His building was up the hill from the riverfront, and Main Street was high and dry. Curious, though, he grabbed an umbrella went to the rooftop of his building and gazed at a barricaded riverfront park. Several streetlights had water lapping around the base. Water covered parts of the park. Walls made of sandbags surrounded the caboose and several park buildings. The flooding was only going to get worse. His director of emergency management had said that northern states had gotten at least ten inches of rain over the last week and more was predicted. All that water in the Upper Missouri and Upper Mississippi River basins had to go somewhere, and that was downstream. Conditions weren't going to be as bad as what had happened in the Great Flood of 1993, which happened before Michael had been born, but all forecasts showed the flooding would be worse than normal.

He returned to his apartment and left the open umbrella to dry. He watched the local news program, whose top stories included the weather and a shooting. After more weather and sports, he stuck around for the closing story. The feel-good feature involved an injured eagle found wandering aimlessly on the ground in southwestern Missouri. However, once the eagle was taken to rehab and x-rayed, rehabbers had discovered that the bird had eaten large amounts of carrion—specifically, the remains of an already dead raccoon—and was simply too fat to fly. After a diet, the bird had been released back into the wild. The reporter relayed that while eagles mostly ate fish, they weren't above passing up a free meal, especially one they didn't have to work for. The reporter also bragged how Missouri had over 400 nests. Michael knew that fact well. He had one of those nests and it was causing all sorts of problems, both professionally and personally.

His fingers hovered over his phone, ready to text Ione

about the overindulgent eagle who'd overfilled his stomach. But then, Michael shoved his phone into his pants pocket. Tonight hadn't gone as planned. He'd come home early to talk to Ione, to confess that he was developing feelings. But instead, he'd discovered her ex wanted her back. And that the permits were caught in the crossfire. And that she hadn't said a word about her relationship. He had conflicting feelings about that.

One, it put his project in jeopardy. But on the other hand, her personal life was hers. If it didn't impact the permitting, then what business was it of his? The only reason he cared was because of his own personal relationship with her. And that relationship still didn't give him the right to question her past or judge her by it. Not if he was asking her to do the same about his.

Michael paced his apartment. He'd always been accused of being self-indulgent, but that was far from the truth. If he was, he'd go see Ione and convince her to give them a chance. Instead, he decided that he would pull back. She'd already indicated her career came first. He had to respect that. He'd let her have space. He'd try to forget her if that's what she wanted. He'd…oh, hell, he didn't know what he'd do. His thoughts were a jumble. For a man who'd always had someone waiting in the wings, who'd been accused of being shallow and who'd had an ex hint at another chance less than twenty-four hours ago, he found himself in foreign territory.

One thing he wouldn't do would be taking Rachel up on her offer. That was over. Michael wanted Ione. Sometimes the worst thing to do was react without thinking, without knowing the full picture. He was in love with her. His heart knew she was it and his head agreed. He sighed, grabbed a glass and pressed it against the dispenser with more force than necessary. He'd play wait and see until he could talk to her. He'd do nothing until he had his permits.

Absolutely nothing, something he'd never done before. Which meant one thing.

Perhaps he'd grown up at last.

Chapter Ten

On Monday, when Ione arrived to the meeting, she discovered Liam in Michael's seat. "Ione, it's so nice to meet you," Liam said as he stood and shook her hand. "Michael's sorry he couldn't be here, but he's on a plane to Memphis today to assess the river and determine if it will impact our hotels as it did the last time it flooded. He should be back later tonight."

"Thank you for letting me know." Ione attempted to ignore the twinge of disappointment flowing through her. Failing at that, she concentrated on the meeting. Michael's absence had one benefit, in that the tension she'd expected became nonexistent. Last night when she'd left Michael and Henry they'd been like two male deer about to lock antlers. Today Henry was all smiles and cordial. The meeting adjourned with agreements on all sides and everyone happy. The governmental higher-ups had video-conferenced in, and they'd agreed as well. The permits were approved.

"Ione, shall we go to lunch to celebrate?" Henry said.

"Oh, she can't." Eva materialized at Ione's side. "You've got to work on PR with me, remember? Did it not make your schedule that you and I have a working lunch? I'll have to speak with your assistant." Eva gave a professional smile and tapped her watch. "Henry, I'm so sorry that this happened. I take full blame. Can Ione give you a rain check?"

"Sure. Text me later," Henry said. As Ione left, she could hear Beverly Jean asking him to lunch so that they could discuss what was expected of her during the nest-removal process.

"Did we have a meeting?" Ione asked as soon as they were out of earshot.

"No. But I do want to eat lunch with you so that we can discuss the matter of my brother."

Ione wasn't expecting that and worry ricocheted through her. "He's in Memphis."

Eva moved briskly and Ione adjusted her stride to match. "While we're a hands-on executive management, we have people who could do what he's doing and report back." They entered Eva's office, a bright, airy room that featured abstract art on the walls.

"Why did he leave then?"

"He left because he didn't want to come between any potentially happy reunion between you and your ex. I, however, have no such qualms."

Ione hadn't been alone with Eva and worry made a knot form in her stomach. She knew Michael had told his sister about the true nature of his and Ione's relationship. But she hadn't expected this ambush. Or the fact Michael knew Henry was her ex. "I took the liberty of ordering in for us," Eva said. "I hope you like pasta."

"Love it," Ione said, because that was easier than feeling like a lamb being led to the slaughter. Eva was the type of woman Ione could never be, a go-getter, the one in charge who could predict which way the dominoes would fall.

"There are sodas and waters in that refrigerator. Grab something and take a seat."

Ione hoped ginger ale would calm her stomach, so she opened a can and sipped. Uncertain what to say or how to act, Ione sat and watched Eva remove multiple take-out containers from a large brown paper bag. Eva handed Ione an empty plate. "There's spaghetti, chicken fettuccine Alfredo and a basil pesto with angel hair. I didn't think you were vegetarian, but I covered all the bases. Help yourself. I don't stand on ceremony." Eva dropped into the seat next to Ione. "There's Italian salad, too."

In the St. Louis region, the ingredients of Italian salad varied, but always contained a lettuce blend, pimentos, Sicilian olives, red onions and chopped artichoke hearts. After Eva took her portion, Ione heaped salad onto her plate. "I always miss this salad when I travel," she said.

"Same," Eva said, passing her the Italian bread that was precut into thick slices.

Ione served herself a small portion of each of the pastas. She placed a napkin in her lap and took some of the real cutlery from the holder sitting in the center of the table.

"I'm glad we have the permits in place," Eva said. "But I don't think I'll release the news until we're ready to turn off the live cam. We don't want any protests."

"Good idea," Ione said. "The pollinator project should give you some good PR in the meantime."

"It will." Eva dipped her fork into her salad. A silence fell as Ione began to eat, too, and as it stretched, stress built. Was she supposed to be speaking? Making conversation? She couldn't read Eva. No wonder she was a VP of PR.

"What is it you want from me?" Ione finally blurted out.

Eva set down her fork. "Michael did say you were blunt. I like it when people are direct, so I'll do the same. I want answers. What is going on between you and my brother? Or between you and Mr. Fish and Wildlife? It seems to me that you've gotten yourself into quite the mess and are in over your head."

"How do you think I feel?" Ione asked. She'd learned that one strategy to handle unwanted questions was to answer with one of her own.

"Are you being sincere or rhetorical?" Eva asked, proving she also knew that technique.

Ione's chest heaved and she pushed her plate slightly forward. "Both. Maybe. I don't know. This is my job. My life. My hometown. I wanted to be here because my mother has cancer and my sister is getting divorced. But then I met your brother and things became complicated."

"And then in walked Mr. Fish and Wildlife." Eva said the words with a such a straight face Ione wondered how she managed it. "Your ex."

"My ex," Ione confirmed. "I didn't know he'd be on this case."

"Michael got the impression that he wants you back. Do you want him?"

"No." Ione could answer that with perfect conviction. "But I can't be with your brother, either. Remember the job?"

Eva leaned back so she could study Ione. "That's the

only reason? My business is reading people. You're hiding something."

"There's a million reasons," Ione told her in the hopes that Eva would let go of this thread. "I'm way older. I don't come from money. I'm socially awkward."

Eva scoffed. "You think my brother cares about any of those things? You're making roadblocks where there are none. I've done it myself at times. It's nothing to be ashamed of. Sometimes the roadblocks are necessary, such as protecting people and keeping them from driving through floodwater. Other times they're things we do when we're afraid."

"I have a lot going on and it's not the right time to have a relationship," Ione said. No way was she getting into her fears regarding cancer, or the fact she might never have children. Then again, if she told Eva, she'd tell Michael, and he'd most likely dump Ione flat. Ione simply refused to wade into those troubled waters.

"That is a fair answer." Eva grabbed her chiming phone. "And I will respect it."

"Thank you," Ione said, noting she had two texts. One was Henry, sending her a link. Cordelia had sent her a photo with the message Is he back with his ex?

The photo was of Michael and Rachel at a gala. The link to the story Henry sent gave the information that the couple had been spotted that weekend in Portland at Margot Van Horn's birthday party. Ione knew who Margot was because she'd stayed in Van Horn hotels before they'd been sold, and because of her research into the Claytons.

"The answer is no," Eva said as if reading her mind.

"A hard and firm no. That photo is not what you think. I was there."

"I wasn't asking."

"But you're thinking about it." Eva began typing rapidly. "I would be. I'm sure that's what Rachel intended, too. It's a great way to get people talking about her again. And what a mess you've all made. Your ex wants you back. Rachel wants Michael. Michael wants you and you don't want him. I'm losing track of all the threads." Eva's fingers never stopped moving. "Thankfully this latest development is pure speculation and there's no damage I need to control. I'm posting the original photograph that shows he was with far more people than how it was cropped. Luckily, I have access to everything."

Eva set down her phone. "Don't let this scare you. Liam and Lexi were far more volatile on social media. She is a pop star, after all."

"Not my world," Ione said. "I live a quiet life. I'm happier laying low."

"Not even if being with Michael can give you everything you wanted? Money? Security? Visibility?"

"Those are the things I want least. I'm content sleeping out under the stars and cooking over a campfire. I don't understand these social dynamics and I don't want to."

"So, no to fame and fortune. Noted." Eva eyed her phone as another notification came across. "Michael is one of the kindest, most generous people around, and I would know since he's my brother. He's a good guy, Ione. He's smart, tenacious and caring. But I'm preaching to the choir. You know this. And I said I'd respect your decision."

"Yes, you did." Ione returned to eating. Leaving food on her plate would be rude, and she was sure she'd already offended Eva by not saying she returned Michael's feelings. She could, though, if she let herself, which she would if things were different. How easy it would be to throw herself into the deep end. Her heart wanted nothing more. But her head overruled it.

The door opened and Liam entered. "Save any of that for me?"

"I did," Eva said easily. "Join us. Ione was telling me about how the pollinator project will be good PR."

"I'm more excited about it saving the bees and other insects," Liam said. "Did you hear that they've found yellow-legged hornets in Georgia? They're an invasive species that threaten the honeybees, which in turn impacts crops. There are traps set all over the state and they're using trackers to find the nests and eradicate them."

With that, the conversation shifted to the pollinator project, and Ione relaxed. Well, somewhat, anyway. Michael's brother was a nature nerd, so Ione found him far easier to talk to than Eva. Liam discussed what he wanted added to the pollinator project scope, and it was almost three before Ione returned to her office, brimming with ideas and excitement.

Liam had mentioned a new pollinator site, one located on the far end of the Grand's property line. While she'd seen other sites, she hadn't seen this one. Since the weather app told her she had a brief window in between the near constant rain of late, she sent a few emails and returned to the hotel, where she swapped out her car for the UTV.

"You have everything you need?" Nicholas asked. Ione had gotten to know the valet well during her brief stay.

"I do." Ione patted her backpack. Besides her normal supplies, she always traveled with an emergency kit, which included not only first-aid supplies, but also protein bars, a change of clothes, and an emergency blanket.

"Stay safe." Nicholas handed her the keys.

"I will. I'll be back in a bit." She'd texted Henry she'd meet him for dinner at seven as they needed to talk. Ione strapped in and put the UTV in gear. The site was located on a far hillside, past both the current golf course and the Chateau. She found the path Liam had mentioned, and the UTV easily handled the muddy terrain. She went down one hill and up the other, the landscape and view simply marvelous.

She then descended and crossed a low water bridge over a small creek that was nowhere close to flooding. The bridge had plenty of height before it would become submerged. The massive oak Liam had mentioned was straight ahead, so she parked and climbed out. The meadow was thick and surrounded by a grove of trees, but it was lovely and out of the way. Liam had told her that Clayton had purchased many of the old farms in the area, especially those whose younger generations had no interesting in farming. "We plan on preserving much of it," he'd said with complete conviction. "Our own natural area."

Ione believed him. Normally developers purchased land for future development use, but not Liam. Michael probably supported his brother wholeheartedly.

Ione pushed Michael out of her mind. She needed to

take photos of the site, make some measurements and get back. Like she'd told Eva, the job was what mattered. She couldn't fall for Michael.

Even if she wished otherwise.

"Thanks, Chris." After returning from Memphis, Michael said goodbye to Clayton's pilot and dodged fat raindrops as he ran to the SUV he'd left in the airport parking lot. He hadn't needed to go to Memphis, but he'd wanted to miss the meeting. He'd wanted space to think. Besides, sometimes the best thing to do was remove yourself from a situation. If Ione was worried about the Clayton permits being held up in unnecessary red tape, then Michael would make a strategic exit. His dad deserved to have his golf course and PGA event. If Ione could be laser-focused on her job, so could he.

That didn't mean he didn't care about her. Fact was, he cared too much. Which was why he was driving to the Grand and not his apartment. Nicholas, who'd kept him informed of Ione's comings and goings—not that he'd asked the man to do so—had texted Michael and told him Ione had taken the UTV out and that he'd expected her to be back by now.

Eva picked up on the first ring. "You back in town?"

"Where would Ione be going in the UTV?"

"Are you stalking her now? That's low, even for you."

He'd debate morals with her later. "Nicholas is like everyone's grandpa. He watches everything and everyone. He said she's not back yet."

"Which is how you knew where Ione was the other night when she was meeting with Henry and why you're treating her like a waif who can't take care of herself?"

"Okay, so it makes me a nosy asshole. And you have no room to talk. You had the doorman track your ex when he was here the night Liam met Lexi. Remember that wedding?" When Eva let silence be her answer, Michael continued. "It's not that I don't trust her. I don't trust him. He doesn't love her. Not the way she deserves."

"The way you love her."

"Exactly." The word confirming his feelings felt good, right. "She's the one, Eva. And if she doesn't return my feelings, it's going to hurt."

"Well, the permit paperwork is signed and delivered. He should be leaving town at some point. Then you can figure out whatever this convoluted relationship you all have is. She saw your picture with Rachel today."

"Good grief. I can't win for losing." He turned the wipers to high. Ione was out in this. "Where would she have gone? Maybe to the eagles?"

"She and Liam were discussing sites for the pollinator project. He was telling her about a site on the old Smith farm. Why don't you just text her and ask her where she is?"

"I tried. She didn't answer."

He heard Eva's sigh. "There you have it. Michael, at lunch she told me that she's not right for you. You need to let this go before it drives you crazy. You want her but she doesn't want you. It's hard, but you'll be fine. You'll survive."

He couldn't shake the feeling that something was wrong. "Is there a way to get to that site from the road? Can you text me the directions?"

"I'm sure she's fine, but sure, if that's why you want."

"Thanks." When his phone pinged, Michael pulled into a gas-station parking lot and retrieved Eva's text. He studied the map. Ione would have taken the quickest route from the Grand. Smith's farm was almost four thousand acres, making it the largest in Beaumont County. It had been Clayton Holdings's first purchase in the area, and the Grand and Chateau stood on parts of the farm's former footprint.

A blast of wind rocked his car, which meant flying a helicopter to the site wasn't an option. He couldn't risk finding the low water bridge impassible, so he'd have to hike in. It was only a mile to the spot once he got to the location of the former Smith homestead.

At the entrance to the place, Michael put the SUV into four-wheel drive and turned onto an unused, overgrown gravel road. Until Clayton Holdings had torn down the buildings, kids had gone there to party. He unlatched the gate and ignored the multiple signs—Smile! You're on Camera! and No Trespassing—that lined the route. He found the clearing where the house had once stood. The only thing they'd left was the 14-by-14 Bavarian-style "she shed" that had belonged to Mrs. Smith. As it had been custom-made, complete with intricate trim, Eva wanted the shed to be moved to the new golf course and used as a drink stop. "What a way to honor their legacy," she'd said. "And good PR."

Michael gathered his windbreaker closer and put the hood over his head. For all he knew, he was about to hike a mile and get soaking wet for nothing. But his gut told him to do it, and normally his gut told him not to do things. This time he was going to follow directions.

* * *

Ione stared at the low water bridge. Not even an hour later, the creek rushed over it. While the UTV was designed for water crossings as long as the water wasn't up to the floorboards, the water was moving too swiftly and the crossing was too narrow. Ione didn't want to risk an attempt. If rushing water could easily lift a car and push it off the road, what might this torrent do to the UTV? The last thing she wanted was for the UTV to slide off the bridge and upend in the creek.

There had to be another way out. She turned around and made it back to the clearing. She stopped and rummaged for her cell phone. She had one measly bar and a low battery so she attached it to the power bank. The wind buffeted the UTV, as if trying to rock it. "I'm not staying out here all night," she said, speaking the words aloud, as if daring Mother Nature to contradict her. She'd been in worse circumstances. She could handle this. But the question was, where to go?

She studied the map she'd downloaded, changing it from street view to satellite view, looking for any road or trail that would lead her to the main road. Most likely she would have to leave the UTV to hike out, but the more she could drive, the better. She located something that looked promising and drove toward it. Coming down in sheets, the rain pelted the roof. She reached the edge of the clearing just as a figure clad in black stepped out. She slammed on the brakes, sending the UTV skidding. But it stopped.

The wipers swooshed as the figure came closer. Ione rummaged in her backpack for the bear spray she kept inside. Then she heard her name shouted at her over the brisk wind.

"Michael?" She dropped the pack and stuck her head out the window as he came round to her side of the vehicle. "What are you doing here?"

"Coming for you. What were you thinking, going out in this weather?"

"The app said I had a window without rain, but when I headed back, the low water bridge was covered. And you're soaked. Get in here."

Michael rounded the UTV and climbed in. A blast of wind came with him. He shook off some of the water, glad the valet had had the foresight to add the UTV's removable cab enclosure. "Thanks."

He was a sight, but her heart swelled that he'd come for her. "How did you know where I was?"

"Nicholas was worried when you didn't return, so he texted me. I'm glad he did. Let's go. We can leave the UTV and take my car back. It's at the old Smith place. It's a bit overgrown, but that path's right through there."

She drove toward where he pointed, the UTV bumping over the terrain. "I would have worked my way out eventually. I've been in worse spots."

"Nothing is happening to you on my watch." Michael gripped the overhead handle as the UTV bounced over a small log. "It makes me feel better when I know you're safe."

"I'm not sure how to feel about that."

"Take it however you want. Okay, one more bend. Here we are." As they came into the next clearing, Michael cursed.

Ione stopped the UTV. "That's not good." A huge tree

had fallen across the driveway, much of its large canopy on top of Michael's SUV. One branch had spiked through the windshield and landed in the back cushion of the driver's seat. Ione and Michael climbed out and surveyed the damage. "It's lucky you weren't in there. You might have been the one needing to be rescued."

"Yeah. That's pretty frightening."

They both silently stared at the car. Had Michael been in the driver's seat, he might have been injured... or worse. Ione fought back the panic. He was with her. He was safe. But he'd come looking for her, and had anything happened to him she would have hated herself forever.

"It's blocking the only way in and out," Michael said.

"Oh." She could see what he meant. There was no way to get around the tree, even in the UTV. "How far to the main road?" Ione asked as they climbed back into the UTV.

"About a half mile or so. We'll need to text someone to come get us." He began sending a message.

"I'm glad you're okay." The thought she could have lost him petrified her. "I'm sorry about your car."

'It's insured. It could have been much worse. I'm going to check and see if we can get into the shed. We left the power on so that we could run the cameras. Keeps the kids from using the place as a party hut."

"Won't it be locked?"

"Yeah, but I've got a master key to every building we own. One of three to everything on the property. Liam and Eva have the other two. Come on. Ready to make a dash for it?"

Ione didn't want to sit in the UTV, especially as

the shed appeared much safer from falling trees. She grabbed her backpack. "Let's go."

Once inside, Michael flipped the switch and the lights came on. "Mrs. Smith was an artist. This was her studio."

"It's cute." While the space was mostly empty, the room had several built-ins, including a long counter and a booth that would seat four. The room also had a combination heater/AC unit set into the wall, like the kind found in roadside motels. Michael turned on the heat. "We're moving this building to the new golf course and using it as one of the bar-and-food pit stops. Most likely near the tenth hole."

Ione shivered. She began unloading her backpack onto the built-in kitchen table. "I've got a change of clothes and I need to take these wet clothes off. You should, too."

"Are you suggesting I get naked?"

"You're in short sleeves and I can see the goose bumps from here. I've got two space blankets in here. I'll even share my food." She lifted her phone. "Great. My power bank is dead and now, so's my phone. I didn't bring the wall charger."

"I managed to text Liam and told him where we are. He said that EMS is already doing two water rescues."

"We don't need rescue. We need a ride."

"Liam said he'll come get us as soon as the road to get here is open. There's a flash-flood warning, so we'll have to wait until that passes."

"Of course."

"The water will recede at some point. Until then,

we're stuck unless we want to walk in this rain and cross multiple fields."

"I've got protein bars and water. We'll survive. I'm changing out of these wet clothes. Turn around."

"You realize I've already seen you naked." But he turned around, and when she'd changed as well, Ione tossed him the two blankets.

"Take off your wet clothes and wrap one of those around you." As he began to strip, she turned around and gazed out one of the small windows. The rain hadn't let up. She slid into the booth, the only place to sit beside the floor. Michael hung his clothes on pegs near the heater and slid in across from her.

"I guess being here means we can finally talk," he said.

"I suppose. We secured the permits today." And without her phone, she had no way to tell Henry that she was would be ghosting him for dinner.

"I'm glad the permits are out of the way. And Liam said to tell you he's sorry you felt pressured to visit this site today. Visiting here wasn't a rush."

"It's not his fault. I'm simply an overachiever who wanted to get a jump on things. I can be too impulsive. Perhaps this wasn't one of my best ideas. I should have known better. I know how unpredictable Missouri weather can be."

"I'd say what am I going to do with you, but I seem to be doing that a lot. And I don't want you to think that there's something wrong with you, because there's not."

Ione pushed one of the protein bars toward Michael. "Then what happened last night? You and Henry acted like two elk in rutting season. I expect that in nature, not from two grown men."

Michael gave her a sheepish grin. "Yeah, in hindsight it was embarrassing and not one of my better moments. But I was jealous and I don't get jealous. Ever. I was out of my comfort zone. But he's wrong for you and I hope you see it. I know I have to let you make own choices. I shouldn't interfere."

His admission shot a thrill through her. Michael had been jealous? No man had ever felt that way about her, including Henry during the entire time they were dating. But she had to keep her perspective. She couldn't let his words sway her away from the course she'd chosen. "I assume that Nicholas was the one who told you I was in the bar."

"Which, as Eva pointed out, makes me a stalker," Michael said. "But in my defense, I wanted to see you. I like you, Ione. I'd figured out something when I was talking with Eva and couldn't wait to share it with you."

She waited for him to say what it was, and when he didn't, she found herself disappointed. Ione hated silence. Even out in nature there were sounds. While the wind howled and rain pounded the roof, their silence created a tension that felt like a bowstring pulled tight. She broke it. "I appreciate all the extras you did for Cordelia's shower. I know it was you."

"I discovered I had some Clayton magic that I could spread, so I did. Jack didn't know that one of his managers had raised the rents, so he's fixing everything. Cordelia should have heard from Jack about her lease. If not, she'll hear soon."

"She already did. Thank you for that. You went above and beyond what I expected when I burst into your apartment that day. That was terribly wrong of me. I never should have done that."

"Ione." Michael spread his palms flat against the wood. "I would do anything for you. Including coming out here to get you. You matter to me. You've rocked my world, and it needed rocking. I wasn't a very likable guy. I see that now. Being with you made me better. Made me do some self-introspection. I'm thankful for that."

Ione rubbed her arms. Was it getting hot in here? She should adjust the heater or ask Michael to do it. "I'm glad I could help. Not that I did anything."

"You refocused me. Made me see things anew. Past me liked the attention. Now, I'm ashamed of who I used to be. Eva told me you saw the picture of me and Rachel. I'm sorry about that. I haven't thought of her in months. It's just you."

His words thrilled her, but a chill still held claim to her heart. She couldn't fall for him. "I don't read social cues well," Ione said. "And after Henry, I have trust issues. He did a number on my head. Still is."

"He told me he made a mistake and he wants you back. So, yeah, I guess we were in a bit of a standoff last night."

"It was awkward," Ione admitted. "I didn't know what to do, and he still had your permits in his control. I was planning on having dinner with him tonight. I don't know what he's going to say, but there's no feelings left on my side. He just wants to settle down because it's time, and he thinks I'll make a good partner."

"That sounds like a business deal. You deserve love, Ione."

Cordelia had said much the same thing. "I do want

something real. Something that is rooted in love. My mom and dad had that before he passed. Sometimes I worry she's not fighting as hard as she could to beat this cancer. But I know she's doing everything the doctors ask, so maybe it's my own paranoia. I don't want to lose her."

"I'm sorry. I'll do anything you want, if it will help."

"It's not your fault, but thank you. I appreciate it." She uncapped some of the water. The action gave her hands something to do, which calmed her nerves. "Anyway, I'd planned to tell Henry tonight that he and I have no future. I don't want a future with him. My career comes first, so I can pay for her treatment. That's always been on me. And I need to be in Beaumont for the length of the pollinator project. Then we'll see where I go next."

"What if you stayed in Beaumont? Why couldn't that be an option?"

"It's on my radar. Which is another reason why I can't start anything with you. What if we don't work out? We'd both live in the same town. I couldn't work with Henry after our breakup. I'm the one who had to leave. I care about you, too. But I can't risk my heart."

Even though he'd heard this before, her rejection still stung. He understood the not-risking-her-heart part well—it was one reason he hadn't told her he was falling in love with her. The other reason was it wouldn't be fair. He couldn't pressure her and refused to guilt her.

While his heart might not have been broken as hers had, he had a heart. He wasn't heartless, like some pundits maintained. He cared deeply about the woman sitting in front of him. Her siren song had lured him in and he'd given her the power to hurt him, a power he'd ceded willingly. He might not have known her long, but he knew her in a way he'd never known another, in an instinctive, basic way, as if they'd been destined for this moment since the dawn of time, as if their DNA wouldn't be happy or satisfied until they'd found each other. Now that they had, the universe was dragging them apart. Michael had never been one who'd paid attention to those posters with the inspirational sayings on them. One came to mind, though: if you love something, set it free. But Michael didn't think if he let Ione free she'd come back, and knowing that sucked. Big-time.

"I understand," he told her. "It's like we're in the right place but it's the wrong time. I wish it were different. That what we feel for each other could be enough."

"Me, too." Ione said. "I can't give you anything more than what we shared." She fidgeted with the wrapper of an energy bar. "Would it be wrong if I said I wanted to be physical again? It would help us pass the time. As long as no one found out, would one more time hurt?"

The last thing he wanted their lovemaking to be was a way to pass the time. But he could deny her nothing. And perhaps this turnabout was the fair play he deserved, for he'd once used women as a way to fill his nights. He'd thought they'd understood the score, but maybe they'd been like he was now, putting on a brave face for one more chance to be with a person you cared about. That thought pained him a great deal.

"If that's what you want." He slid out from the booth and stood. Unashamed of his nakedness, he unwrapped the blanket and spread it on the floor. Wordlessly, he held his hand out. He'd make this last time as perfect as he could, something to remember when the nights grew dark and lonely, and his newfound maturity reminded him there were worse things than being alone, and one of those was to treat sex as a frivolous hobby, as he once had.

She walked toward him, her hands working to undo the buttons of her shirt. He captured one of those hands and drew her close. He didn't want a quickie or something clinical. He wanted to kiss her until she moaned, until she could bear no more. He wanted to brand her with his mouth and show her he loved her without using words. Then, and only then, would he allow her clothes to fall away. His mouth found hers and he nipped gently, the lightest of butterfly kisses. He savored her like fine wine, sipping the heady sensation of her pleasurable sighs. He kept her hands pinned tight within his grip. Tonight was about her pleasure. He'd give her everything words couldn't say.

Time ceased to have meaning in moments like this. He stripped her and lowered her to the floor. He lay her head on the second blanket, which he'd folded into a tiny makeshift pillow. He lifted her arms above her head. "Don't move them," he told her. "If you do, I'll stop."

He wouldn't, but he wanted her exposed like a decadent feast on which he planned to dine. Her chin dipped in acceptance. Her body was a smorgasbord for his senses, and so he indulged, tasting his way from her breasts to her core. He thought nothing of his own need, or how much he wanted to feel himself sheathed deep inside her. Instead, he took his sweet time, bringing her to orgasm after orgasm.

Her hands found his hair as she disobeyed him. He lifted his mouth. "What did I tell you?" he warned.

"I don't care. Enough. I need you now. My turn."

Ione was strong, not surprising since she was an athlete, and as she wrapped her legs around him Michael found himself rolled onto his back. He didn't mind. Above him, her skin was flushed. A light sheen of sweat covered her cheeks. She straddled him, so close to what they each wanted. "Take me," he told her, because he was hers. "Do it."

She wasted no time shifting. He'd been ready this entire time, and a surge of triumph cruised through him as she settled atop. She set the pace, and he somehow held on to his sanity as if it was a thread tightened to the breaking point. He'd last as long as she needed, come hell or high water, which perhaps was appropriate, given their current circumstances and location. But then, his thoughts dissolved into nothingness as passion stripped away everything but the essentials of two becoming one. He wouldn't say the words, so he let his body show how he loved her. It was there in the way his hands held her hips, in each thrust, and in the way he held her closely to his chest once they'd both flown beyond the horizon.

"That was…" she whispered as she rested on his chest.

"Yeah," Michael agreed, his hands stroking lightly over her back. A thesaurus wouldn't have enough words to describe how wonderful and transcendent their lovemaking had been. Because it *was* lovemaking, not sex.

She shifted onto her side, nestling her head into the crook of his arm. He ran a fingertip down her nose.

"If I fall asleep you'll wake me, right? Because I want to do this at least once more."

"Me, too." *And a million more.*

She snuggled deeper and closed her eyes. He pulled out the other blanket and covered them with it. "Get some rest, sweetheart."

Tomorrow would arrive far too soon.

Ione woke to the sound of chainsaws. Sunlight streamed through the small windows. She clutched the blanket to her chest and sat up. She was the only one in the cabin. It was morning, the rain was over and Michael's clothes were missing.

She dressed quickly. Her rain-soaked outfit from the previous day was almost dry, so she shoved it into a waterproof section of her backpack. Her stomach grumbled. She and Michael had eaten all the food and water she'd brought. She'd lost track of how many times they'd made love and how many orgasms she'd had. Michael was proof positive that the third time was the charm. She was securing the top button of her shirt when he walked into the shed.

"Hey. You're awake," he said. He stood a distance away, as if respecting the cold light of day.

She wished she could go to him. "Heard the chainsaws."

"Some of the Grand's grounds crew is here. The road's passable again. As soon as they get us free, we'll drive back in the SUV they brought. They'll load the UTV onto a trailer and the tow truck will get my car. About fifteen minutes tops before we're out of here."

Reality had returned and she didn't like it. "I'll be ready."

Michael handed her the power bank he was carrying. He took a cord out of his pocket. "I had them bring that for your phone, since yours was dead."

"Thank you."

With that, he disappeared back outside and Ione plugged in her phone and noted it was almost 9:00 a.m. She'd slept far past her normal wake-up time, probably owing to her and Michael's nocturnal activities. She had two bars of service and her messages began to arrive. Most were from Henry, who became more and more irate as he realized he'd been stood up. Then the tone changed: Eva sent me an email saying you're stranded by the flooding. Sorry I've been a jerk. Would take the messages back if I could.

He'd sent nothing asking if she was okay. Biting her lip, Ione sent a quick text: I'm fine, thanks for asking. Michael came to rescue me.

She could see the bubbles, as if he was typing, but no reply came. Probably for the best. She sent messages to her mother and Arwen before she gathered her things and stepped outside. Down the lane, she could see the UTV being loaded up. Another flatbed tow truck had Michael's SUV strapped to the back. The tree had been cut away and big chunks sat on each side of the drive. Michael came toward her. "Ready?"

"Yes." She followed him to the Grand's SUV and climbed inside. After locking the shed, Michael joined her in the back and the driver put the car in gear and took them back to the hotel.

The driver parked under the portico and a valet

opened the door. Michael turned to her and pushed some of her hair aside. "Don't worry about going into the office. Most of us are sandbagging today. The river's supposed to crest late tomorrow, and as long as we don't get any more rain, the town escaped major damage."

"I'll work from here. Thank you again for coming and getting me."

"Anytime." He held her gaze a second longer than necessary before he broke the contact.

Ione stepped out of the car and watched as the driver left, taking Michael who knew where. She felt as if she'd just lost something precious. Then she saw Nicholas. "I should be mad at you. But I do appreciate you worrying. However, no more telling Michael my whereabouts."

"Yes, ma'am. I'm glad you're okay. That storm was pretty harrowing."

"It was, and thank you." She went up to her room and set her backpack down. She took a shower, dried her hair, dressed and ordered room service, which arrived quickly. Once she'd eaten, she opened her laptop to check email. As she finished up the last of anything needing immediate attention, she found herself yawning. She'd take a short nap. Maybe twenty minutes, tops. However the nap turned into hours of much-needed sleep.

Which was why, Ione learned later, she missed the start of the firestorm about to erupt.

Chapter Eleven

"I'm glad you're okay." Eva ran her gaze over Michael, which made him uncomfortable. He should have stayed at home rather than going into the office. Too late now. "Is Ione coming in?"

"I told her to work from the Grand. She didn't get much sleep."

"You mean you both didn't get much sleep," Liam said. The three siblings were sitting on the couches in Michael's office.

"We didn't," Michael confirmed, his tone serious rather than giddy. He had no reason to celebrate. "It was more of a goodbye than anything. She doesn't want to be with me."

"That sucks. I'm sorry, bro," Liam said.

"Me, too." Michael lifted his third cup of coffee. It might be nearing noon, but he needed the caffeine to stay awake. Letting go of the woman he loved had drained his energy. "Which is why from here on out, you're running point where she's concerned. You're the firm's environmental warrior, anyway."

"That I am, and, yes, I will," Liam said. "Happy to

do it to help ease your pain. And I don't mean that with sarcasm, either."

"Appreciate the clarification." Michael checked his frustration before he banged his fist on his leg, which would make him hurt more. "I finally find the person who could be the one, and the only thing she wants from me is sexual. And don't say it. I'm well aware that I was usually the one saying those words to women."

"Lexi took some convincing. She didn't believe that I was serious," Liam said. "She kept thinking I could never love her because of what I'd shared with Anya. But we got past that. She realized how strong she was and was able to fully open her heart."

"Ione's strong enough. She's sure of herself. She's simply saying no because she has other priorities."

Eva squeezed Michael's hand. He appreciated the comforting gesture. "We're here for you."

"Thanks. Tell me that Henry's gone and that our permits are secure."

"Yes to both," Liam said. "He and his cohorts should be on their way to Minneapolis as we speak, and Beverly Jean has headed back to Jefferson City to the conservation department headquarters."

"Dad knows that we're good?" At least one person would be happy.

Eva nodded. "He does. We had breakfast with him while you were being rescued and he's pleased. You did well, Michael."

The words should have provided comfort, but Michael took little pleasure in them. He'd done his job, one he'd never asked for. "Do you think Edmund's ever coming back at some point?"

"Are you tired of working with us?" Eva asked. "You're a really good VP."

"I feel adrift, that's all," he admitted. "Beaumont won't feel the same."

"Understandable," Liam said. "You went from the Portland Playboy to Mr. Responsible. You've done everything asked of you, including moving here. The change hasn't been easy."

"I don't mind stepping up," Michael said. "I've enjoyed many aspects of the job. But my personal life has done a complete flip. Not that I'm going back to before."

"I'm sure some scandal will come along again," Liam teased.

"Let's hope not," Eva said. But, as if Liam's declaration had tempted fate, her phone began to ding. She swiped and began to read.

"What's wrong?" Michael said upon seeing her frown.

"Who the hell took a picture of you tucking Ione's hair behind her ear?"

"What?"

"This morning. There's a photo of the two of you in the SUV at the Grand this morning. If it's staff, I'm firing someone." Eva turned her phone around so that Michael could read the headline: Environmental Consultant Spends Night with Clayton Playboy.

Michael cursed.

"Wasn't an employee, from that angle," Liam said. "We had some national reporters and freelance photographers staying with us to cover the flooding. Might have been one of them."

"Probably." Eva read the photo credit. "The photographer's not one I recognize, but he sure found a buyer quickly. This should blow over. It's all smoke."

But when there's smoke, there's fire, which was how Michael's past and present collided two hours later, when his sister charged back into his office to tell him the story had grown from his and Ione's night together. Now, it included the upcoming removal of the eagles' nest. "I haven't even released this information. Did Ione say something?"

"She wouldn't, and she hasn't answered my texts," Michael said. "We need to protect her. She's still in the hotel. Security never saw her leave her room. I have a feeling she's asleep. I would be."

"I'm working on a press release now about the nest removal," Eva said. "Get Liam in here."

"He went to help sandbag." Michael said.

"Of course, he did." Eva paced. "Text him and tell him we have a situation. He's the best person to handle media like this. People trust him."

"I'm already here," Liam said as he strode into Michael's office. "I'm up-to-speed if the townsfolk asking me about the eagles means what I think it does."

"Several environmental groups are berating us and calling us conspirators," Michael said. "That we pulled a fast one so that we can build a golf course."

"I can address that. I'll say we want the eagles to move the nest to the new nature reserve. Can we expand that by another ten acres?" Liam asked.

Eva was already typing on her phone. "No, we can't. Not unless we buy the farm next door. We have an option, but they don't want to move at this point."

"The designer said last time there's no more wiggle

room. We have to give Dad his tournament." Michael tried to ignore the sinking feeling in the pit of his stomach.

"We also need to talk about the pollinator areas at all the wineries," Eva told Liam. "Ione sent you a draft of that, and while it's not perfect, it's close enough for general talking points."

"But what about Ione?" Michael asked.

"We say nothing. We redirect back to our key message. I'll handle that part," Eva said.

"And Ione? What should I tell her? This is going to devastate her."

"The truth." Eva held Michael's gaze. "That a whole lot of things, things she's not going to like, are about to hit the fan and make her life a nightmare."

Ione awoke to someone pounding on her door. She blinked awake. The clock read a little after four. She climbed out of bed and opened the curtains to discover that clouds had rolled back in. She walked into the living room.

"Ione, are you in there?"

Not Housekeeping, but Michael. She opened the door and he rushed in. "Are you okay?" he asked.

She worked out a kink in her neck. "I was asleep. You really should stop stalking me like this. I'm fine."

His worried gaze searched her face. "Then you haven't seen the news. You need to sit down."

"Now, you're scaring me." Knees wobbly like a colt, she sat in one of the armchairs as Michael brought her some water. "What's going on?"

"You. Me. We're all over the news. I'm not going to sugarcoat it. It's bad. It's the last thing you wanted."

"Show me." Realizing she'd silenced her phone, she discovered multiple messages from Michael. She also had a scathing one from Henry not fit for human consumption.

"I just sent it," Michael said as her phone pinged.

She clicked the link and rage filled her as she read the speculation. "Tell me Eva is on this."

"She is. Liam will be talking about the environmental concerns. We aren't saying anything about us."

But it didn't matter. It looked bad. Even if it could be argued that they were just work colleagues, those opposed to the nest removal were calling for a review.

Ione read a quote and her fingers tightened. "I can't believe he did this."

"Henry?"

"Who else? Did you read what he said? I rejected him so this his narcissistic way to show me he's still in control. How could I have been so stupid to have fallen for him?" A savage shake of her head didn't fix her anger. "All this because I rejected him?"

Michael dropped into a chair across from her and clasped his hands in his lap. "It is not your fault. It's mine. I shouldn't have gone to the site. I'm the one who set this into motion."

She should have anticipated that Henry was never going to take her rejection well, and she'd made it worse by sending him that text.

"Listen to this." She read his quote. "'While the removal of the nest will move forward, in the future Clayton Holdings would do well with disclosing its conflicts of interest, as should Good-4 Environmental.' What a jerk."

Michael took her cell phone from her clenched fingers. He set the device on the side table. "Don't read any more."

"What makes it so bad is that it's true. We did sleep together. What must everyone think?"

"That it's not your fault. Stop beating yourself up."

As if fate wanted to make a mockery of her career and add injury on top of insult, her phone began to ring. Seeing the caller ID, she snatched her phone from the table and swiped. "Hello, Norman."

She'd known this call from her boss was coming from the moment she'd seen the headline. Wondered why it had taken this long, especially as the article was hours old. "Yes, I understand," she replied after listening to what her boss had to say. "I'll start packing."

Michael frowned. "Where are you going?"

"I'm wanted in Atlanta. Good-4 will be sending someone else to finish the pollinator project."

Michael couldn't believe it. "No, that's not acceptable. I'm going to reach out and..."

Ione's hand on his arm stopped his tirade. "Please, don't make it worse. It's best for all parties, both of our companies, if I go. You know Eva would agree. There's no need to try to be a hero."

The resigned expression on her face, the sadness there, nearly broke Michael in two. This situation wasn't fair. "I..." He was at a loss.

"Please," Ione said softly, her tone a knife plunging into his heart. "Let me handle this. Just go."

He hated this. Felt powerless. "Can I at least have Chris fly you back to Atlanta?"

She shook her head. "They're emailing a ticket. It's best I travel commercial. Thank you for everything." She stuck her hand out and Michael took her hand in his. Unable to help himself, he pulled her to him. She didn't resist. He rested his forehead against hers. "I am going to miss you."

"Same." Her admission caused a shudder of resignation to run through him, so he hugged her tightly. As she began to pull away, he released her. If he kissed her, he'd be lost. And he wouldn't insult her by asking her to quit her job and stay with him. Ione wasn't that type of woman. She'd find that solution offensive and condescending. Instead, he'd do what she'd asked. Again. Always.

He walked away, her stricken and hopeless expression burned into his mind. As soon as he was in the hall, he called Eva. "Good-4 Environmental is recalling her to Atlanta. We have to do something."

"Michael, you have to lay low. Do not do anything. Do you hear me? Do nothing."

"They're going to fire her. You know that."

"That's a worst-case scenario." Eva was ever the optimist.

"You know that's the *exact* scenario. She needs her job and bonuses to pay her mother's medical bills. She'd hoped to get this bonus so she could pay for an experimental treatment for her mom's cancer."

"So you do it," Eva said.

"What?" He'd thought of it, but knew Ione would never accept charity. "She'll refuse."

Eva's voice came clearly through the line. "Don't tell her it's you. Edmund sent Lana and her entire family to Paris. It was technically a bonus from her boss, Wendy Cederberg, but he arranged it."

"I didn't realize that the trip was a bonus."

"That's because you weren't VP yet and were in Portland. Edmund wanted to make Lana happy even if she'd never love him back. Let me contact the hospital. Even with HIPPA regulations, we should be able to get things done. This is Beaumont. The town takes care of its own."

Michael's decision was instantaneous. "Do it. I want Ione to have one less thing to worry about, especially if she loses her job. Which will be entirely my fault." He heard Eva sigh. "What? You know it's true. There has to be a solution."

"There always is, but let's calm the media first. Liam's press conference starts in about fifteen minutes."

"I'm on my way."

Once Ione checked out of the Grand, she took a rideshare to Arwen's. Nicholas assured her he'd return the rental car and that, no, doing so wasn't a problem. Ione's plane didn't leave until almost nine, so she had some time before she had to leave for the airport. Unable to help herself, she watched the local news. The story about the removal of the eagle nest took the third spot at the top of the hour, right behind the updates on area flooding. Liam handled the interview with ease, answering every question with authority. Everyone knew how pro-environment Liam Clayton was, so if he promised the eagles would be fine, then they would. The head of one of the local groups doing the protesting said they were satisfied with Liam's answers, and that he'd invited them to be present during the nest removal, to which they'd agreed.

Crisis averted. One problem solved.

But Ione's issues were just beginning. She knew she'd be jobless once she returned. If worse came to worse, she could tap into her 401K, but she'd prefer not to do that. Hopefully, once the scandal died down, she'd find another position. She had some paid vacation accrued, and surely she'd get some sort of severance.

"You could always come home," her mom said, as if reading Ione's thoughts. They were the only two sitting in the family room as Arwen had taken Paris to dance class and Roman was upstairs doing homework. She'd already said her goodbyes to them.

"I'm going to be fine," her mom insisted. "You can't keep living your life to take care of me, Ione. At some point, you have to let go and trust in the universe."

"You know I don't believe in that."

Her mom rubbed the fuzzy blanket she'd draped across her legs. "Which is why you need to get yourself tested. Do it before you lose your insurance. Do it for my peace of mind, if not yours. It's been hanging over your head and holding you back for years. It's time to know."

"I'll get it scheduled when I get back. I promise."

"Good. If they can get you in, you'll have the results by the wedding."

The doorbell sounded and Ione admitted Cordelia, who was Ione's ride to the airport. After some brief chit-chat, Ione hugged her mother extra tight and bade her goodbye. Through the passenger-side mirror, Ione could see her mom remained in the doorway until Cordelia turned left at the end of the street.

"I'll watch over her," Cordelia said. "You okay?"

"Honestly? No. This isn't how I expected to leave."

"Henry's lucky he's already gone, or he'd meet me in some dark alley." Cordelia smacked the steering wheel for emphasis. "And I won't ask you what you're going to do because I know you don't know."

"I'll figure it out. My mom asked me to get tested. I'll do that for her."

"About time. And what about Michael?"

"We talked last night. It's not going to work."

Cordelia risked some side-eye. "Ione. He's clearly besotted with you."

"I gave you all my reasons."

"And I'm not saying they aren't valid. But at some point you have to let go and take a leap of faith."

"My mom said something similar. But the universe doesn't work like that."

"Stubborn to a fault. What if he loves you?" Cordelia lowered the radio volume. "You are lovable, Ione. I want you to think about that this week when everything feels bleak. I love you. Your mom loves you. Arwen loves you, as do Paris and Roman. I have a feeling Michael loves you, too."

"But he's never said it."

"Ione, I'm not an expert on men, as clearly my ex is a jerk who quit and ran the moment things got rough. But I can safely say that men are often idiots. Foolish when it comes to matters of the heart. Michael's probably as scared as you to take a leap of faith, especially as the two of you haven't even had a real date. You also told him it would never work before it even started."

"It doesn't matter now," Ione said.

"Well, think about it. And don't forget, you're back in town for wedding week. I expect you to be here that Tuesday afternoon. No excuses. Melody and Denise are arriving then, too."

Melody was an intellectual property lawyer who worked in New York City. Denise was an actress flying in from LA. The foursome had hung out together in high school and once they'd graduated, Cordelia had kept in touch.

"I'll be there," Ione said. "This will not make me miss your wedding. I'm looking forward to seeing everyone."

Cordelia put the car in Park, letting it idle in the passenger drop-off so she could hug Ione across the center console. "Keep me posted. I'm here if you need me. Always."

Ione bit back the tears. "I will." Before she broke down, she climbed out and grabbed her luggage. Time to go home and face whatever came next.

Which, in the end, while bad, wasn't as terrible as it could have been. Good-4 Environmental did indeed fire her Thursday afternoon, but they provided three full months of severance pay, including insurance, and paid her for one month of vacation. "I'm sorry we have to do this," Norman said. Her now-former boss sat behind his large desk, with Ione in the chair in front of him. "You've been one of our hardest workers. I'll say that when anyone calls me for a reference. Cork and Bantry have been trying to steal you for a while. I'd give them a call. I don't believe your indiscretion will bother them in the least. I'll put in a quiet word."

"I appreciate everything you've done for me," Ione told Norman. "You've been a great mentor. And I'll reach out once I'm back from the wedding in about two weeks. I'll have a better picture of what I want to do then. Maybe Cork and Bantry might be a fit."

Norman tilted his head. "You know I'll help you in any way I can that doesn't hurt the firm's reputation. Just let me know. And what will you do before you leave for Beaumont?"

She'd saved enough airline miles and had enough hotel points. "I think I need a head-clearing vacation. I've always wanted to hike the Grand Canyon."

"You should. I miss the days when I could get out in the field. It's the best high there is, and I should do it more. You take care, Ione."

She didn't cry until she got home. Afterward, she booked a flight to Arizona and took things one day at a time.

She hiked the South Rim. She completed the entire 12-mile Plateau Point section of the Bright Angel Trail. She'd pushed her limits on the round-trip hike, which had given her views of the inner canyon and its formations, and taken her almost eleven hours. The way back had a difference in elevation of 3,080 feet, but wildflowers had been in bloom, as if Mother Nature was promising good things to come.

After her minivacation, Ione flew back to Atlanta for her medical testing. On Tuesday, it was back to Beaumont, where she discovered her reservation had been modified to a heavily discounted room at the Blanchette Inn. "You didn't have to do this," Ione told Mrs. Bien.

"Don't make a fuss," Mrs. Bien chided as she handed Ione her key. "Beaumont takes care of its own, and we all know how much you've been doing to take care of your mother."

Mrs. Bien bustled Ione up the stairs and ushered her into a room with a glorious canopy bed. "You just enjoy staying with us, okay? Breakfast is at eight. And we're having a happy hour downstairs, so please join us."

Ione set her suitcase on the stand and glanced around. Wallpaper consisting of a cream background and tiny pink roses adorned the walls. The trim was dark wood, as was the bed. The canopy was also cream, as was the matching bedspread. She freshened up in her private bathroom and went downstairs. Mrs. Bien had light appetizers on the dining room buffet and a variety of wines and cans of sparkling water. "Help yourself."

Ione selected a mango-peach-flavored water and filled a plate with cheese, crackers and carrot sticks, then took a seat in the parlor.

"Here you are!" Cordelia entered. She was staying at the inn as well, to be near her bridesmaids. She snagged a glass of champagne. "Mrs. Bien told me you'd arrived."

"I was about to text you."

"Sure you were," Cordelia teased. She flopped onto one of the couches.

"Well, after I ate something," Ione admitted.

"Better," Cordelia teased. "You know you can't lie to me. You're the first to arrive, but Denise should be here soon, and Melody arrives later tonight. She was in court all day, so she's on the last flight out."

"Can't wait to see everyone," Ione said.

"Me, either. So have you seen him?"

Ione knew exactly whom Cordelia meant. His apartment was just two blocks away. "I just got here."

"Have you spoken to your mom?"

"What part of 'I just got here' did you not hear?" Ione asked.

"Ooh, you made a joke. I'm impressed." Cordelia tipped her champagne flute back and drained the contents. "I assume you haven't spoken with Arwen, either."

Mrs. Bien refilled Cordelia's glass. "Mrs. Bien, you should tell her. Your husband is on the city council."

A loaded look Ione didn't understand passed between the two women. Mrs. Bien smiled. "You know how the town always has its annual trivia night? Well, the city decided to use the money raised to fund your mother's treatment."

"You know, the experimental one," Cordelia continued, as bubbly and upbeat as the sparkly golden liquid in her glass. "Isn't that great? It's done, Ione. Paid for. She'll start in two weeks."

"But how? Why? The town needs those funds. Especially after all the rain we had. The riverfront park flooded and needs reconstruction."

"The town will be fine," Mrs. Bien said. "The flooding means we're eligible for a bunch of grants that will pay for the repairs. The merchant association also came through. We love your mom, Ione. Let the town do this for you."

As Ione's tears welled, Cordelia grabbed Ione's hand. "It's okay, Ione. I told you, things work out. Now, let's get this wedding week officially started. Get rid of that water and join me in a toast. After all, as the maid of honor, it's your job."

"Yes, ma'am." Ione took the filled flute Mrs. Bien passed over. She clinked it to Cordelia's. "To you and the best week ever."

* * *

To no one's surprise, the next few days flew by. Wednesday night was a dinner at Miller's Grill for the wedding party, and both the bride and groom's parents. Thursday evening the bridesmaids took Cordelia out to eat while Will and the groomsmen went into Chesterfield to Top Golf. During the days, there were final dress fittings, wedding guest favors to prepare, makeup and hair trials, and meetings with the wedding planner to coordinate final details on things such as flowers, food and reception music. Not once during the times Ione and Cordelia were at the Chateau did they see Michael.

Ione looked for him, though. She couldn't help it. Her curious nature hadn't let things rest, and at one point Will had let it slip that Jack Clayton had made a huge donation to the city coffers following the flooding, including money to restore the underside of the caboose, which had taken on some floodwaters.

"So that's why the town could help my mom," Ione said. Will's reply had been an "uh" and he'd quickly changed the subject.

Ione could follow the breadcrumbs, and she finally confronted Cordelia as they readied to leave the inn for the wedding rehearsal. "Did Michael pay for my mom's treatment?"

"What are you talking about?" Cordelia sat on a stool in front of an antique vanity. She brushed mascara over her eyelashes, and Ione moved behind her.

"Don't lie to me." Ione put her hands out. "If you do, I'm going to mess up your hair."

"You wouldn't dare!"

"Try me." As the words came out, Ione wasn't sure

if she was joking. "Besides, you and I promised no secrets. Remember that pinkie swear back in kindergarten? And sixth grade?"

"Fine." Cordelia closed the mascara tube. "Michael came to me two days after you left."

"What! You didn't tell me this. So much for no secrets."

"Hello. You were in the Grand Canyon, remember?" Cordelia slid off the bench and out of Ione's reach. "He feels really guilty about what happened and knows you'd never let him help. You're too proud and stubborn. So he and his siblings came together and gave the money to Jack so that it would cover what the city needed, thus allowing the city to help your mom, who, by the way, doesn't know, either. You can't tell her."

"I won't. And this is so convoluted. But you and Will know," Ione pointed out, overwhelmed by what Michael had done.

"Because he came to me and asked. And the Biens know. And maybe the city administrator. But the rest of the town thinks the funds came from a really good trivia night. You would have liked it. Lots of science questions."

"Why would he do this? We haven't even been on a date."

But Cordelia didn't answer. She was already out the door, Ione on her heels, to meet the other bridesmaids downstairs for their ride to the Chateau. The rehearsal took a half hour, as it was a quick run-through, with the minister explaining how things would go tomorrow during the actual ceremony. Despite it being a dry run, Ione still had tears in her eyes as Cordelia, carrying her bridal shower bouquet made of ribbons, took Will's arm and walked down the aisle.

The rehearsal dinner was in the Chateau's Library, an actual library with wooden bookshelves running the room's perimeter. The Chateau had brought in long tables to seat the thirty people in attendance. Candelabras, white linens and fine china place settings helped to create an intimate atmosphere.

"I feel like I'm in Downton Abbey," Melody said.

"Wrong country," Cordelia said with a laugh, "but I know what you mean. It's perfect." She turned to Ione. "Thank you."

Ione didn't know what to say, so she said nothing. This was all Michael. Sure, she'd badgered him, but he'd done this for Cordelia because of her. He was a good man and she'd let him go. Worse, she now knew she was in love with him. Not because of what he'd done, but because he'd done it expecting nothing in return. And for a whole list of other reasons as well.

Her feelings remained the same the next day, when Ione joined Cordelia and the rest of bridal party in Room 37, a sumptuous suite, to dress for the wedding. Ione had never been so grateful for waterproof mascara, especially when massive tears flowed down her face as Cordelia and Will said their vows.

After making sure her makeup had survived the deluge, it was time for pictures, and another delicious meal. After Will and Cordelia had their first dance, Ione wandered off, not wanting her melancholy to infect the joyous occasion. She loved Michael. Maybe had from the moment she'd met him and asked him to take her home. They were H_2O. $NaCl$. Better together than apart.

But would he accept an apology? Would he see her if she tried to find him? She had to try. She followed a gurgling sound to a large fountain set in the center of the French garden. A tall, beautiful marble woman poured water from a Grecian jug. The figure was surrounded by cherubs, or nymphs—Ione wasn't sure which. Besides the water pouring from the jug, in the basin below the woman other waterspouts formed arches. Ione sat on the edge and dipped her fingers into water that was baby bear porridge perfect—not too hot, not too cold.

"Hello, sea nymph." The voice made Ione jump, and water splashed over her bridesmaid's gown. "I see you've found Aphrodite."

Ione's chest heaved and she worked to calm herself. Michael stood there in a casual suit jacket, the top two buttons of his white shirt left undone. He looked divine, like a Greek god come to life. "Is that who this is?"

"Edmund had her commissioned especially for this garden."

"But the Chateau isn't Greek."

"Art's art, and she is spectacular."

"That she is." Ione rose. "Were you looking for me?"

"Actually, no. Not this time. This moment happens to be by chance. This is one of my favorite spots, and I'm on my way to the reception. I had time to pop by. I guess it's fate you're here, like that night we first met."

"Ah. I see." When he made to step away, Ione decided that maybe she should seize the moment. "I believe I owe you a thank-you. I know it was you behind my mother's cancer treatments."

He gave her half a whimsical smile. "There are no secrets in this town, are there?"

"Will accidentally let it slip and then Cordelia told me. I mean, I did badger him a bit, and he'd had a beer or two, and she's my best friend, so it's not their fault."

"You can't let things go, can you?"

"No. I always need full information." She paused before boldly pushing forward. "But there some things I do regret letting go, you being one of them. I'm sorry that I hurt you."

"I'm a big boy, at least last time I checked. I'll be fine."

He wasn't opening up to her like she'd hoped. Could he forgive her? "Maybe so, but you put yourself out there and I didn't believe you meant it. That's on me and I'm sorry."

Michael shoved his hands into his front pants pockets. "First, I never do anything I don't mean. Especially not where you're concerned. Second, you have nothing to be sorry for. I keep telling you that."

"But I do. I was so afraid that I'd turn into another woman you discarded that I couldn't let myself believe what you and I had might be different. I knew Henry had ulterior motives for wanting to take me back. What I didn't know was yours. Why me, of all people, when I wasn't even worthy of a jerk like Henry? And that fear meant I threw obstacle after obstacle in your way. And you gave to me freely, anyway, without asking for a thing in return." She gestured toward the sky. "Cordelia's wedding. My mom's treatment. Cordelia's shower."

"It's good business. Being good neighbors."

He hadn't shocked her or sent her scurrying, but his dismissal made her angry. Ione had no idea where this burst of surety about her love for him came from, but as certain as she was that the sun would rise in the east tomorrow, she was certain Michael's nonchalance was deliberate, and that it was up to her to break through the walls he'd erected around his heart. "You know it's more. *I* know it's more. You did it for me. Admit it. Don't lie to me. For once, let's be honest with each other."

"Yes. I did it for you. Because I wanted to make you happy and I've never cared about making anyone happy before. Well, except for myself. I want one thing. You, Ione. *You*."

His declaration sent a powerful jolt through her. Okay, this was it. The moment that would decide everything. "I have to tell you something. It's big. Maybe I should have told you earlier. I don't know if I can have children. I might have the genetic markers for the same kind of cancer my mom has. I'm also older and that means I'm more at risk for pregnancy complications. Before we go any further, I need to tell you that."

He took a step and stopped. "Is that one of the reasons why you kept saying no?"

"Yes. No. I mean, yes, it's why I said no. You deserve to have a wonderful woman who can give you everything. Children. Family. Forever. Right now, I don't even have a job."

"What I want is you, Ione. *You*. I'll tell you that as often as it takes." He crossed the gap. He took her hands and warmth fused their fingers together. "I'm in love with you. I see a future with you. If that means we don't have children, we don't. If it means I sit with you in the hospital—let's hope not—I will. I love being with you. You are enough. More than enough on your own. As for a job, you'll find one. I'd never presume to think you're with me for my money. In fact, just the opposite. You want to work, you work. I'll support you in anything you do."

Which filled her heart with joy. "You know the right things to say."

"Do I? Because with you one can't be too sure. I feel like I bumble things when I'm around you."

"Which is why I'm in love with you. You make me happy. You support me. You see me."

"I will always see you." He ran the back of his fingers along her cheek. "You will never cease to amaze me. Does this mean you'll finally go on that date with me?"

"Yes. But I don't know if I can wait. Maybe, since there's a reception going on, we could have our first dance now?"

"I think that can be arranged. But now, I have to come clean. I wasn't going to the other reception. I just didn't want you to think I was some pathetic lovesick fool who was hovering around the Chateau looking for a chance to talk to you."

Her heart felt so full it was like a dam about to burst. "I'll let you in on a little secret myself, but from now on we can't have secrets."

"Fair enough. What is it?"

"When you found me I was sitting here figuring out how to go find you."

Michael's grin split wide. "And that, sweetheart, is why we're perfect together." He circled his arms around her. "I'm going to kiss you now and then we'll go dance."

Ione turned her face toward his. "Sounds like a plan."

"It's not just a plan. It's a promise."

And as his lips found hers, Ione felt something she'd

never experienced before in a kiss: love. He loved her. She loved him. He showed her in every nip, in every delicious swipe of his tongue.

Hand in hand, they headed back to Cordelia's reception.

"Here you are! It's time for the bouquet toss!" Cordelia rushed to Ione the moment she stepped back under the tent. "Michael!" Cordelia gave him a huge hug that almost knocked him back a step. "I love my wedding and reception. I love this girl. You take care of her, okay? But right now I need her so you'll have to wait." She turned to Ione before he could answer and pointed at her. "You, come with me."

Ione found herself shuffled onto the dance floor, where the single women jostled for position. Ione glanced around. She hated these things, so she eased her way to the far edge of the circle. Cordelia would throw up and straight backward, so if she stood over on this side, she should be safe…

Except Cordelia decided to intentionally lob the bouquet in Ione's direction. And Ione's instinct from years of volleyball was to bump it back. But before she could, a hand shot out and grabbed the base. "I believe this is yours," Michael said. He winked, amusement and affection on full display.

Ione took the bouquet and inhaled the floral fragrance. Cordelia rushed over, a large grin on her face. "You're wicked," Ione told her best friend.

"You know it." Cordelia took the bouquet and set it on a table. "Go dance."

A slower number began, and Michael gathered Ione

in his arms. "I guess this means you're the next to be married?" he asked.

"That's the thought behind the tradition."

He kissed her gently, pulled back and smiled, letting her see all the love he had in his eyes. "Then it's a good thing we're on our first date."

Epilogue

"Dr. Clayton! Dr. Clayton!"

Ione glanced in the doorway of her office. Her administrative assistant, Carolyn, stood there. "I knocked. Twice."

"I didn't hear you." She wasn't used to her new last name, either. It had been two weeks since she'd married Michael in a small, intimate ceremony in the Chateau, on the anniversary of their official first date. They'd taken a week-long honeymoon in Costa Rica, where Ione had hiked to her heart's content—well, when she wasn't making love to her husband. "What's going on?"

"Have you checked the eagle cam?" Carolyn could hardly contain her excitement. The eagles had returned to the area in January, and as Ione had predicted last May, the bonded pair had built a new nest in the conservation area. "We have babies! They're hatching!"

"Why didn't you lead with that?" Ione cued the live feed. There on the screen was the first eaglet. Next to it, the second egg was cracking as a beak began to break through. "Does Liam know?"

"He's the one who sent me to get you! He's in the conference room, watching on the big screen."

"Tell him I'll be right there." Ione sent a message to her husband that he was needed in the conference room, stat.

Her husband. She liked the sound of that. Michael worked two floors up, as he was still a VP. His job duties had expanded, though, because Liam had declared that he wanted to work on the company's philanthropic endeavors and environmental affairs. He'd been the one to contact Ione. She'd had an email in her inbox the Monday morning after her reunion with Michael. Actually, Liam had sent it on the Friday of Cordelia's wedding rehearsal. But Ione had been too busy with wedding week to check email, so she'd missed it.

She'd also missed the notification from her doctor's portal. When she'd checked that Monday morning, she'd learned the happy news that she didn't have any of the genetic markers for the cancer. She hadn't realized how heavy the weight on her shoulders had been until the words of her doctor had lifted the burden away.

Grabbing her cell, she headed to the conference room. The screen with the live feed took up most of the wall, and she could see thousands of people were online watching as the eaglets hatched, and the number kept growing. Eva would be thrilled with the good PR.

Michael came into the conference room and wrapped his arms around her from behind. She turned her face so that she could kiss him. "Hey."

"Hey." He couldn't help himself and gave her another kiss. He glanced at the screen. "That's incredible."

"Lexi's got the girls watching from home. They might not remember it, but…" Liam was beside himself. "This is her calling now." With that, he left the room.

Since Ione was the head of Clayton's environmental division, she saw a lot of Liam and Lexi, his Grammy-award winning wife, who had since become one of her close friends. Lexi had even performed an impromptu concert at Kaiser's, testing out her newest song. It had been Lexi and Cordelia who'd helped Michael propose to Ione, keeping his secret and giving her the best surprise—an engagement ring on a Halloween ghost tour for family and friends led by Arwen. To this day, most on the tour swore they'd seen the Woman in White during the proposal, but Ione thought that the reality was simply tears and misty weather. But it made for a good story.

She'd also learned that some secrets were best kept secret, at least until they were ready to be shared at the right moment. Not that her bluntness allowed her to choose the right moment. Especially with Michael talking sweet nothings in her ear. "So incredible. You knew they'd come back."

"I know something else, too." She wiggled around so she fully faced him. "I have a secret."

"Since we promised that we could only keep good secrets, I assume it's a good one."

She couldn't help herself. Happy tears began to fall. "The best. I promise. I just love you so, so much."

"And I love you. We're bonded like those eagles. For life." Then his gray eyes widened. He could always read her, and he knew what she wanted to tell him without her saying a word.

She nodded in confirmation. "Nine months incubation and we'll have one of our own."

He whooped and lifted her off her feet. "I'm going to

be a dad," he told everyone in the room. After the cheers, he kissed her again. "I love you."

"And I love you." She captured his lips with hers.

"I'm the luckiest man in the world."

Which made her the luckiest woman. Always and forever.

Just as nature intended.

* * * * *